Lenormand Thirty-Six Cards:
Fortune-Telling with the Petit Lenormand

An Introduction
by Andy Boroveshengra

Copyright

Text copyright © 2014, 2015 A. Boroveshengra.

All rights reserved. No part of this book may be used or reproduced in any manner whatsoever, including Internet usage, without written permission from the author, except in the form of brief quotations embodied in critical articles and reviews with the appropriate citation.

As the purchaser of this e-book, you are granted the non-exclusive, non-transferable right to access and read the text and graphics of this e-book on screen in the format purchased.

The text may not be otherwise reproduced, transmitted or downloaded. Any unauthorised usage of the text is a violation of the author's copyright and is illegal and punishable by law.

Cards: 1880 Dondorf © A. Boroveshengra.

Additional Graphics: © 2014 D. Howard.
Astrology Chart: © Traditional Morinus [used with permission].

Dedication

This book is dedicated to my nieces and nephews and to all those who work with the Petit Lenormand, and all those who wish to learn how to read with the cards.

Acknowledgements

First and foremost, I thank my ancestors: Their lives, stories, sacrifices and love never go unnoticed. Remembering them is the first step to understanding myself.

I would not have been able to write this book without the prior tuition of my mentors, Aunt Elisa and Euphemie Al-Ansari. You are with me every time I spread these cards. Thank you.

I owe much to my mother and father who taught me the importance of belonging and being your own man, and much more. Thank you.

This book would never have been written without the assistance of my siblings. Thank you.

My dear friends Ioan, Luke, Dotty, Dawn, Tina and Bryan all supported me both when I first wrote this book and during this revision. I am eternally grateful to each and every one of you.

Olayinka, your wisdom and mentorship flow with such generosity that I doubt I can ever repay you. Thank you. Ase-o.

I must pay tribute to several individuals who have supported and helped me in various ways: Stella Waldvogel, Michelle Ross, Ciro Marchetti, Lidiya McCabe, Nadia Sokolov, Vivianne Kacal, Alison Cross, and Margaret Patterson. Thank you.

To Chanah Morrison, Björn Meuris and Angela Shikany: Thank you. I wish you well wherever life takes you.

To Malkiel Rouven Dietrich, Iris Treppner, Erna Droesbeke, Marie Marco, Britta Kienle, Claire Seifert, Mario Dos Ventos, Rana George and Caitlín Matthews, who have preserved these methods by their work, I salute you. I hope with humility that my book may assist in bringing new readers to the works of these authors and others more knowledgeable than I.

To Robert from Morinus for kindly allowing me to reproduce an astrological chart with their software.

To my editor Tara: Thank you.

To the Cartomantes' Cabinet classes of 2013–2015. So much of how this book has been written was influenced by you. I thank each and every one of you. Keep dealing the cards!

To Nathan, who was the first person to suggest I write a book.

And to She who has protected me, healed me and guided me, *Sara, voliv tut mai*.

Foreword by Alison Cross

With 20 years of experience and a long family history of Romani readers, Andy Boroshevengra stands out amongst the current crop of Lenormand practitioners and authors. Taught by his aunt when he was only a child, this book contains insights that only great experience and familiarity with the cards can bring.

This 3-section book distils everything that you might need to get started with the Lenormand deck: keywords and meanings, themes (people, animals etc), how to combine the cards, and, of course spreads.

The Spreads section opens with the 36-card Grand Tableau, but newbies need not feel daunted. Andy not only breaks down the spreads into manageable portions, but also leads the reader step-by-step through a series of worked examples in a self-assured and trustworthy voice.

There are also 10 Appendices to this book that are exceptionally useful to both the beginner and experienced reader alike.

Alison Cross
Chairman of the Tarot Association of the British Isles (http://www.tabi.org.uk)
Scotland, United Kingdom
June 2015

Preface to 2015 Edition

The truth is that when I asked my Aunt Elisa to teach me how to read the Petit Lenormand, I did so solely because I was struggling with my palmistry apprenticeship. My childish reasoning was that these thirty-six slightly twee-looking cards could not be as difficult to master as the intricacies of palm reading, and, when I was finished, I could devote myself to what I wanted to do.

To my initial chagrin, I discovered that I was completely wrong. The Lenormand is an oracle of depth and complexity, and it played to two particular boyhood interests: cryptology and stenography. I was hooked.

That fascination has not abated. I still enjoy laying the cards and deciphering their meanings. It is also client sympathetic – my clients can participate and 'see' my workings and delineation in a way they cannot with palmistry. For me, that is important. Unlike some, I like that my clients can see how I arrive at an answer or from where I derive my conclusion.

The emblematic representations of the Lenormand are universal in a way that other cards, such as the tarot, are not. Unlike the lush representations of the Visconti-Sforza or the esotericism of the Thoth deck, we can all immediately recognise and understand what emblems like a child, a dog or a heart signify.

There is an accessibility to the Petit Lenormand which defies its age and allows it to syncretise easily with our modern lives. We can see how the message of the Letter can come to us by way of fax, text or email just as we can see how the Ship could also represent an aeroplane.

This, too, is important to me: It allows for precision and clarity, and it removes the need to negotiate a plethora of esoteric possibilities that one card can often hold in other systems. Now, I am not against esoterica or the occultists' stance on card reading, but I favour the common-sense, precision and down-to-earth nature of classic cartomancy.

Thus, this book is a traditionalist tome, but I class myself as an evolutionary traditionalist; meanings evolve naturally with usage. What does not work gets thrown out.

Writing a book on the Petit Lenormand was not something I planned on doing. I had written enough about it on my blog and authored a very well-received course. What more could I say? I found that as Lenormand's popularity continues grow in the Anglo market, the more documented method of reading Lenormand continues to become far too rigid and confusing, with set cards meaning work and sex, et cetera. Readings are still becoming abstract, vague and watery.

I believe this is because concrete definitions were replacing the multi-variant, constructed meanings of the method of distance and attendance. Whilst distance seems very complex, it is actually quite versatile and not heavy on rote. It is all about engagement. If the Fish is near your card, you engage directly with it. Money is near you. If it is far, then you do not. You're in a financial draught or have got to go some distance to get your money.

This concept of engagement – near and far – is vital to manipulating the cards in contextually specific ways that give real, concrete and individual-specific answers.

In the original preface to this book, I said that this method had all but vanished in literature in Germany, Holland and France. I no longer believe this to be true. Proximity has not been explicitly referenced, but books are littered with references to combinations and conventions which derive not from modern insights but the earliest methods (proximity). Proximity is the lynchpin, but it remains regretfully absent from the emerging English-language market.

Because of its immediacy, the Petit Lenormand has a broad scope. Questions can be answered. You can use it to tell fortunes or to discover what is set to happen in a specific area of life. This book will teach you how to do that.

Others use it to talk to the Ancestors, the Orishas and the Saints.

Whatever your aim may be, the method of using these cards can be worked into your goals and practices. The Lenormand's inclusivity never ceases to amaze me. While it started life as a game aimed at the bourgeoisie, Petit Lenormand found a home with the damen who read to make extra money, the savvy doamnelor of Eastern Europe, and even the mãe-de-santo of Brazil. It is my hope that it will amaze you, too, and that it will enrich your life.

Teboslowil tut o-Del.

Andy Boroveshengra
Redditch, United Kingdom
May 2015

Table of Contents

Copyright..2
Dedication..3
Acknowledgements..4
Foreword by Alison Cross...6
Preface to 2015 Edition..7
Table of Contents...10
Introduction..15
    What Is Petit Lenormand?...16
    History of the Petit Lenormand..16
    Cartomancy with the Petit Lenormand Method....................18
PART ONE: The 36 symbols and their meanings.....................22
The Meaning of the Four Suits..23
    HEARTS..25
    SPADES..27
    DIAMONDS...29
    CLUBS..31
The Meanings of the 36 Cards..33
    1 – The Cavalier..35
    2 – The Clover..37
    3 – The Ship...39
    4 – The House..41
    5 – The Tree...44
    6 – The Clouds...46
    7 – The Snake..49
    8 – The Coffin...51

9 – The Bouquet	53
10 – The Scythe	55
11 – The Rod	57
12 – The Birds	59
13 – The Child	61
14 – The Fox	63
15 – The Bear	66
16 – The Stars	68
17 – The Storks	70
18 – The Dog	72
19 – The 'High' Tower	74
20 – The 'Forest' Garden	76
21 – The Mountain	78
22 – The Paths	80
23 – The Mice	82
24 – The Heart	84
25 – The Ring	86
26 – The Book	88
27 – The Letter	90
28 – The Lord	92
29 – The Lady	94
30 – The Lily	96
31 – The Sun	98
32 – The Moon	100
33 – The Key	102
34 – The Fish	104
35 – The Anchor	106
36 – The Cross	108
Exercise #1 – Reference Sheet	110
Card Themes	**111**

- Communications 111
- Love 111
- Family and Home 112
- Happiness 112
- Work 113
- Finances 113
- Warnings 113
- Sickness 114
- Trouble 114
- Animals 115

Exercise #2 – Themes 116

- Exercise #2 – Themes (Answers) 117

Positive to Neutral to Negative 118

People Cards 120

PART TWO: Combining and Reading the Cards Together 123

Building Combinations 123

- Proximity – Being near to or far from the significator and other key cards 125
- Attendance – By what cards it is touching 128
- Exercise #3 – Attendance Practise 134
- Exercise #3 – Attendance Practise (Answers) 136
- By Direction 138
- By Correlation 140
- By Theme 143

PART THREE: Laying the Cards 145

Spreads 145

The Traditional Grand Tableau 146

- How I Read the Traditional Tableau 148

- Additional Techniques..152
- Example Reading..159
  - Step One...159
  - Step Two...159
  - Step Three..161
  - Step Four...161
  - Step Five..164
  - Step Six..165
  - Step Seven...166
  - Step Eight..167
  - Step Nine...168
  - Step Ten...169
  - Outcome...178
- Grand Tableau Worksheet..179
- The Past, Present and Future Grand Tableau.................181
  - How I Read the Past, Present and Future Tableau......182
  - Discerning what is 'Past' and what is 'Future'............184
  - Important Information..189
- Example Reading..191
  - Step One...192
  - Step Two...192
  - Step Three..192
  - Step Four...193
  - Step Five..194
  - Step Six..196
  - Step Seven...197
  - Step Eight..198
  - Outcome...202
- Fan Spreads..203

- Daily Readings...204
- Exercise #4 – Daily Draws...206
- Yes or No..207
- Lines of Five..209
- Lines of Nine...212
- 3 x 3...217
- Pyramid Spread..229

Conclusion..236

Appendix #1 – Describing People..238

Appendix #2 – Health Combinations...................................249

Appendix #3 – Playing Card Meanings & Multiples........255

Appendix #4 – Timing...259

Appendix #5 – Grand Tableau Houses...............................265
- Game of Hope Houses...265
- Game of Hope House Meanings....................................267
- Master Method..269
- Master Method House Meanings....................................269

Appendix #6 – Learning Resources....................................273
- Online Resources...273
- Books...274

Appendix #7 – Translation of the 'Philippe Lenormand' Meanings..276

Appendix #8 - Decks..283

Appendix #9 – Combination Readings...............................285

Appendix #10 - Mademoiselle Marie-Anne Le Normand 292

Andy Boroveshengra...297

Introduction

Just a few years ago, most of my clients would not accept Petit Lenormand readings, preferring palmistry or tarot, with which they were familiar. It is only over the past decade that Lenormand reading has come to the wider attention of the English-speaking world. With the rise of the Internet, card reader and collector communities have engaged more and more with the pack. It has also become far easier to obtain decks.

Petit Lenormand has been immensely popular for over 150 years in Europe, especially in its native Germany and continental and Eastern Europe, and it has a huge following in Brazil. There are books in German, Dutch, French, Spanish and Russian but only one book was published in English before the millennium (Erna Droesbeke's *The Oracle of Mlle Lenormand*). Sadly, Droesbeke's book has been out of print since the late 1990s. A second book, Mario Dos Ventos' *The Game of Destiny*, would not be published until 2007.

What Is Petit Lenormand?

Contrary to popular belief, the Petit Lenormand is a method of reading rather than an actual deck. Specifically, it is a method of reading a stripped deck of Alemannic playing cards. Most commonly, this method is now employed with a special set of cards, which we refer to as Le Petit Jeu Lenormand. However, it can be done with an 'ordinary' playing card deck. This method arose from the use of a Central European pack of cards most common in the 18th and 19th centuries in Austria, Germany, Hungary, Switzerland and parts of Eastern Europe. This pattern, sometimes called Alemannic, is comprised of hearts, bells, leaves and nuts (sometimes referred to as acorns).

We look further at the role of these suits played in the method in part one of this book.

History of the Petit Lenormand

On her death in 1895, Lady Charlotte Schreiber bequeathed her large collection of fans and playing cards to the British Museum. Included in this substantial collection was a set of cards named *Das Spiel der Hoffnung* (The Game of Hope). Das Spiel der Hoffnung was invented by the German brass-factory owner, Johann Kaspar Hechtel, as a parlour board-game. This board-game is the earliest surviving example of the deck of cards now called Petit Lenormand.

An older deck, known as the *Viennese Coffee Cards*, has been proposed by American author and tarot reader, Mary K Greer, as the ancestor of the *Das Spiel der Hoffnung*; however, this remains unsubstantiated by any of the surviving primary sources. We should also remember that the emblem books contain many, if not all, of the same symbols.

In the middle of the 19th century, *Das Spiel der Hoffnung* was transformed into the Petit Lenormand, re-titled after the famous French fortune-teller, Mademoiselle Le Normand, whose celebrity clients included Marié Josephe Rose de La Pagerie, later, more famously known as Empress Josephine, the first wife of Napoleon Bonaparte.

Why this reinvention occurred, we do not know. The classic answer is that Le Normand's celebrity status proved attractive to card manufacturers. This stand is supported by some examples that were published under the name of other celebrity diviners. However, another theory states that a copy of the Petit Lenormand was found in an inventory of her belongings after her death. Sadly, there is nothing to substantiate such a legend.

From the mid-19th century, several versions of the Petit Lenormand were produced, primarily in Germany and Belgium. These were exported widely to both Scandinavian and Slavic countries. The popularity of certain designs saw them frequently copied, such as the Dondorf (produced by Dondorf Frankfurt, and reproduced in this book).

Whilst numerous designs were produced between 1860 and the 1920s, over 90% of decks utilise the same instructions. These instructions are currently best known as the 'Philippe Lenormand' sheet, owing to some editions being signed by this fictitious 'heir' to Mlle Le Normand. It was reproduced in German, French, Dutch and English and exported to Eastern Europe and Scandinavia as well as North and South America.

Of note is that all books published prior to 2000 use meanings derived from this sheet, which formed the foundation for the Brepols deck's poems, which were later translated into Dutch, German and English.

A translation of this sheet is included in the appendix of this book.

Cartomancy with the Petit Lenormand Method

Cartomancy with the Petit Lenormand utilises much of the pre-esoteric fortune-telling conventions and reading methods. It is direct, no-nonsense and versatile. I disagree strongly when some call it non-spiritual, negative and mundane. However, I do not see the spiritual as divorced from the mundane (worldly), nor have I ever found readings overly negative. Its usages and limitations rest solely with the reader.

Prior to the 19th-century occultists, few if any fortune-tellers used tarot cards, which were still expensive. Instead, the salon mesdames invariably used regular gaming cards. The size of the decks varied from area to area and reflected the most popular games.

Few books were ever published on parlour fortune-telling; instead, the readers invariably learnt from one person and supplemented this oral knowledge with common sense, practice and life experience. Readings invariably used all-card spreads laid out in rows and relied on quick techniques such as counting, pairing and noting how cards fell in relation to each other. These are all things we see in the Grand Tableau.

The majority of literature produced on the Petit Lenormand was and remains in German. The first non-German language book was *Petit Lenormand: Méthode de Cartomancie* by Tunisian-born Italian Marie Marco.

As the Petit Lenormand has not been the subject of such a gigantic amount of literature as the tarot, the methods employed with it have remained remarkably consistent with those popularised by the few books published in each country.

This is part of the difficulty this method of card reading has faced. Whilst individuals could acquire several packs of cards, the absence of literature in English obscured the method of reading those cards. Zealous individuals took to the Internet and various online translating services to cherry pick information from websites and forums, and myths grew.

The most enduring myth is that the Petit Lenormand method is about memorising hundreds of card combinations. This is not true. There is also a notion of 'schools' based on using certain cards to identify work or sexuality. This is not true, either.

You will not be asked to memorise lists; nor will you have to worry about schools' meanings. There are no such things. Not all readers in Belgium use the Moon for work, just as not all French readers use the Fox. As you will see, the cards are multi-variant, so there is no singular card for employment, et cetera.

I learned to read the cards from my Aunt Elisa, and I later had the good fortune to have a few lessons with a woman who had learned in Paris in the 1970s. Although they were born in different countries, in two very different cultures, the two women read more or less in the same way. I have since liaised with readers in Russia, Romania and Brazil, who also read virtually the same way, with a few idiosyncrasies.

The ideas in the following text are firmly rooted in my teachers' insights, but my understanding has evolved over the years of my professional practice. Your understanding and use of the cards will build on what you first learn, too.

Ever since Aunt Elisa first showed me the cards, I have been fascinated by them. Twenty years later, I am still a student. I have written this manuscript in the hopes that it may help to dispel a few rumours and provide a relaxed and easy-to-follow introduction to the traditional methods of reading the Petit Lenormand deck.

These methods are proximity (based on the cards' distance from each other in a reading) and combination. The card order of A + B is not the same as B + A. Combination reading is done using the meanings of the card symbols rather than what the pictures on the cards appear to be doing or remind you of.

I also wish to stress that I make no claims, here or elsewhere, that my ethnicity or the fact that I learnt from someone else, rather than a book, makes me a better teacher or reader. It is just how I came to learn. As stated above, my understanding has evolved over time. Several of the best readers I knew learnt from books, or on their own. However you come to fortune-telling, dedication and practice is what will make you a 'good reader'.

When you have finished this book, you should have a thorough knowledge of the Petit Lenormand. I would encourage you then to look at further avenues of exploration, by authors such as Malkiel Dietrich and Iris Treppner (German), Caitlín Matthews and Rana George (English), and Erna Droesbeke and Björn Meuris (Dutch).

My utmost hope is that the method proves both as fascinating and useful to you as it has to me.

PART ONE: The 36 symbols and their meanings

The Meaning of the Four Suits

The Petit Lenormand – to the best of our knowledge in 2015 – started life as a game called Das Spiel der Hoffnung, or The Game of Hope, invented by Johann Kaspar Hechtel. It was first published sometime between 1798 and 1801. In his instructions, Hechtel noted that the cards could be used not only for the board game he designed but also as an ordinary playing card pack, most likely to play *Schafkopf* (a German game) or *Jass* (a Swiss game) or to tell fortunes.

Hetchel included on his cards the two most common variations of suits found in what is now modern-day Germany, Hungary and Austria. The top left showed Bavarian suits, and the top right showed Alsatian. The former is more common in south-eastern Germany, Austria, Hungary and parts of Eastern Europe. The Alsatian suits were common in West Germany, Switzerland and the Alsace region of France and looked identical to French suits.

Bavarian, or Alemannic, playing cards have suits commonly called hearts, bells, leaves and nuts. These correspond to the suits of hearts (hearts), diamonds (bells), spades (leaves) and clubs (nuts) in Anglo-French and Alsatian packs. In Alemannic cards, rather than queens or jacks, there are over- and under-knaves, respectively. Since the reunification of Germany, in an effort to differentiate the Alsatian pattern from the Anglo-French packs, playing cards have been printed with 'yellow' diamonds and 'green' spades (leaves).

The above is an important fact. The Petit Lenormand divinatory system is based on reading thirty-six Alemannic (German, Alsatian and Swiss) playing cards. Much of the individual cards' meanings derive from their suits. All 'bad' cards are found in the malefic suit of clubs. Thus, Petit Lenormand is a Germanic example of the Italian Sibillas cards, the pictorial playing cards. In any reading using between five and fifteen cards, you can note the suits. More clubs: a time of difficulty. More spades: growth. Seeing the two together would emphasise difficulty in growth and happiness.

I will now delineate the traditional significations of the Alemannic and Alsatian suits. For clarity, I will use the Anglo-French suit names.

HEARTS

Unlike Anglo-French cartomancy systems, where a significator is often drawn from the suit associated with the querent's complexion, the card which represents the querent in Central and Eastern Europe traditions is generally found only in the Hearts cards. For a man this is the König (King) and for a woman the Ober Knabe (Over-Knave = Queen).

Hearts are often also the 'key' suit in that all the Hearts cards deal with the querent's domestic affairs, daily life and immediate surroundings. Unlike Anglo-French conventions, the Hearts is also a 'masculine' suit. This seems to be based on older chauvinistic concepts.

We do, nevertheless, find a masculine association: the Ace is the Lord card, which always stands for the male querent. The King and Queen of Hearts, who are known as the House and the Storks, are the two senior 'domestic' cards in the pack, which deal with the querent's home and changes to home life, respectively.

The Cavalier card, similarly, deals with news coming to the home or, when far away, potentially related to the querent's household or having an indirect effect on one's day-to-day life.

The other key significations found within this suit's themes are wishes and sincerity of affection. The idea of sincerity is found predominantly the Dog card but also in the Moon card, which deals with how one is recognised and thought of, especially professionally but also socially and among one's peers and community. The professional aspects of the Moon card deal with our career on a day-to-day basis and how we are flowing and experiencing our professional lives.

Obviously, the Heart card deals with love, which is not exclusively romantic but also platonic and familial. Our romantic relationships are actually found explicitly in cards from the Spades suit.

Both the Tree and the Stars cards deal with wishes and personal happiness. The former is always the card of the querent's body and overall health, but when it falls with the House, the Garden, the Road and the Sun, it has traditionally been seen as sign of a wish being fulfilled (it also offsets any sickness). The Stars card more directly shows your personal aspirations being fulfilled.

Hearts is also the suit associated with spring, with the magyar kártya (Hungarian cards) variation specifically showing the Ace as spring.

SPADES

This is the suit that often confuses everyone! Spades are bad, right? Wrong. In the Central European pattern, Spades were not seen as a blade but as either leaves or shields. The shield in question is more of a crest, indicating status and privilege. This suit deals with the most generative areas of life, such as relationships, hopes, and all things that make life worthwhile and cause it to flow easily.

So, a Spade primarily represents our happiness and the things from which we draw pleasure. In the Petit Lenormand, this is shown by the King and Queen of Spades – called the Lily and the Bouquet – which signify happiness at the innermost and day-to-day levels, respectively.

As mentioned above, in reference to the shields, often the cards within this suit reveal people of the querent's own age and within his or her social circle; for this reason, we see the inclusion of cards such as the Child, the Garden and the Letter here. These deal with how well we are thought of, our social activities and our communications, respectively, among people with whom we interact. In the case of the Garden, these are typically people we want to be around and want to belong with!

It's also the suit that shows how happy we are made by those to whom we are attracted. Obviously, during the 19th century, this was presumed to be a member of the opposite sex, but, in this day of equality, those attracted to their own gender will derive their happiness from the ranks of Spades. Specifically, this is the Lily and the Anchor, which show the ardour and depth, respectively, of feeling in your lover.

Another theme associated with this suit is one's hopes for the future and future endeavours. We see this within the Ship and the Anchor cards, which also show the successful growth, especially financially, of our projects. The Anchor (9 of Leaves) is the 'big hope' card.

This is also the female suit. Obviously, we get that with the inclusion of the Lady card as the Ace.

As the suit of youth and vitality, it also contains the Tower card, which shows our life and, hopefully, the attainment of old age and lasting happiness.

Spades is the suit of autumn, which may seem strange, but this was the season where how fruitful your endeavours were mostly became evident in relation to the harvest's yield.

DIAMONDS

It would be quite easy to guess that the suit of Diamonds would deal with matters concerning one's prosperity, but it is also the suit of the precarious nature of life and one's individual cares and concerns. Are you struggling with day-to-day life? Diamonds will tell you that. When they dominate, we see stress, a need to be cautious or that your shoulders are too burdened.

But let's get the money side over with first!

Within the Diamonds' ranks are found the two key financial cards: the Fish and the Coffin. The latter might surprise some Petit Lenormand readers, but the oldest signification of the Coffin includes financial losses, not just sickness, and I've found the financial meanings to be the more frequent augury in day-to-day practice. Often, it's a sign of 'dead money': making just enough to dent the credit card bill, paying out 95% of your salary on bills, et cetera.

In the more general sense of fortune, we have cards such as the Sun and the Key, which both grant and withhold success with blockages and insurmountable obstacles. Far away, these are quite difficult cards and often ensure that everything that can go wrong does.

Alongside this general sense of affluence, there are cards which deal with how carefree life is. The Clover card grants a sense of joy and companionship or grief and loneliness, while the Road and the Book can bring interesting interjections and revelations that can go either way. The Road can also show a magical opening which allows difficulties to be escaped from, thus underpinning this suit's unpredictability.

There are also some very difficult cards such as the Scythe and the Birds, which augur danger to the querent and sorrow when near. The former becomes more indirect when it is far away but is never nice.

The Diamonds cards do not belong to any gender.

Diamonds are generally held to be the suit of summer. This fits with the inclusion of the Sun card but also with original symbol – a small bell – which was frequently worn as ornamentation during the summer revelries.

CLUBS

Clubs (or, to use the older name, Flowers) are often seen as positive by Anglo fortune-tellers, but the Alemannic suit is quite different. In the Clubs' ranks, we find the most difficult and negative cards. Clubs signify the unpleasant occurrences of one's life, from dishonest folk or individuals with power over us, to misfortunes and grief, and traditionally – if they engulf the significator – sickness, although I have found this more often refers to unhealthy situations, not physical ailments.

Consistent with the Germanic emblem for Clubs (acorns), and its association with serfdom, the Club cards contain meanings associated with people who might have or who aim to acquire power over us. The Rod, the Bear and the Fox all have these nuances. The Bear can indicate someone with sway over us, or can often indicate people close to home who turn on us due to envy at our good fortune, which is what it predicts. The Fox represents our rivals or people who seek to exploit us for their own gain. With the Fox, this can often refer to employment issues, but it does not specifically deal with the success or failures of our careers. The Rod disturbs our household with strife and contention or sickness.

The Mountain shows us our greatest foes.

Of particular note is the inclusion of several cards that indicate deceitful people. These are the Snake, the Fox and the Mice, which deal with matters as diverse as betrayal, exploitation and theft.

This dichotomy of good and bad tidings is also found in the inclusion of the Ring, which is one of the relationship cards. So why is it here? Frequently, the Ace of Clubs would show a surprise that could be pleasant if it was with Hearts and Spades but would otherwise be negative. The Ring brings joy or sorrow to our relationships.

Within this method, the most unpleasant card is the Clouds. This card has the ability to blacken and disturb most – if not all – of the other cards and exacerbate other malefic ones. The thirty-sixth card of the Petit Lenormand is the Cross, which is also found in this suit and symbolises hardships and grief.

Winter is the season associated with the Clubs. This is the leanest time of year, where our households are often disturbed by sickness and extra financial burdens such as heating costs.

The Meanings of the 36 Cards

This part of the book outlines the cards' meanings. Different decks ascribe different names to the cards. I receive a lot of messages about why I call certain cards by certain names. Subsequently, after much consideration, the names used in this edition are all translated from the original instructions.

For each card I have included:

1) A single word that encapsulates the card's essence, plus three simple keywords that give the card's basic meanings.

2) A summary of the card's traditional emblem.

3) The traditional card meaning denoted by its proximity to the significator card and to the Clouds.

4) A more in-depth delineation of the card's importance, as well as progressed meanings, based on my experience.

5) The basic health significance of the card.

I must remind you that the cards cannot be used for diagnostic purposes, and to do so would likely result in prosecution for the illegal practice of medicine (even if you are a doctor, nurse or psychologist in most countries).

Nevertheless, the Petit Lenormand oracle is such that some health topics will often appear, so I include the health meanings to be complete. If you see something in a reading, encourage the person having the reading to seek proper medical advice.

After the card meanings I have included themes, which put together cards that share a topic, followed by a ranking in terms of positivity. Finally, I list which cards can appear as people. You should learn these associations.

1 – The Cavalier

9 of Hearts

Keywords:
News, a man, vehicles

News is the essence of the Cavalier card.

Normally, the Cavalier's emblem is that of a young, dapper and virile man riding astride a horse on the road. Depending on the deck, he can be shown riding left or right.

The primary meaning of the Cavalier is news. When it is far away from the significator, the news has traditionally been seen as coming from abroad or a place some distance from the querent's home. In contrast, when close to the significator this is indicative of news from one's neighbourhood, or even from someone within the home or family.*

In itself the Cavalier is a positive card; however, the nature of the news it brings is denoted by the cards surrounding it. With the Clouds or other auguries of inauspicious influence, the news will cause some sorrow or trigger hard times.

Progressed Meanings:

The Cavalier can represent a man set to appear in your life. When the Cavalier is describing a person, it will be an up-and-coming, well-dressed and often athletic individual. He is an intern in the big city, the man on the up at work.

Close to the Heart, the Ring or the Lily, the Cavalier can show a new male love interest. The Cavalier is also the same-sex partner card for a man.

The Cavalier stands for one's personal mode of transport, from a bicycle to a car. It can also denote a horse.

As a fast-paced card, the news it brings is rarely a long time in coming. It also signifies positive developments and the need to act quickly. Carpe diem!

Health: The Cavalier shows an improvement in health matters. It also symbolises all ligaments, the legs, knees and ankles.

* In the majority of readings these days, I have found that the news the Cavalier brings, when it is far away, is non-family related or does not directly affect the querent (a boss gets engaged, a friend is made redundant) rather than from abroad. In contrast when it is near the news is often 'close to home' or family related.

2 – The Clover

6 of Diamonds

Keywords:
Joy, companionship, luck

Joy is the essence of the Clover card.

Sometimes, decks show the flowering clover plant in full, but more simple decks normally portray the easily recognisable four-leafed clover symbol.

The Clover symbolises happiness and joy. Quite often these are derived from our surroundings, so there is a promise of comfort and companionship in this card, too. When it's located near the querent's card, and free from negative influences, you can expect bad times or loneliness to lessen.

This, however, is reversed when the Clover is located in the vicinity of the Clouds or other negative cards, which can see anxieties increase and difficulties appear or worsen. When it's far away from the significator card it can often show loneliness, depending on the severity of the cards surrounding it.

Progressed Meanings:

As with the Bear and the Fish, the Clover can represent money. However, unlike the Fish, the Clover most often represents smaller amounts, usually under £100. It can also signify your wallet and piggy-bank, so do beware seeing the Fox or the Mice near it.

Just like the Sun, the Clover's good fortune can be doubled by the presence of the Birds. Remember that the Clover is a simple and short-acting card, so seize the opportunity it brings and enjoy it while it lasts.

In a timing question, the 'when' of the Clover is anywhere from three or four days to a month at most.

Health: The Clover usually shows a recovery and a pick-up in our mood or energy. When combined with cards of sickness it tends to indicate deficiencies of minerals and vitamins, especially those we get from vegetables and fruits.

3 – The Ship

10 of Spades

Keywords:
Travel, trade, longing

This card symbolises the essence of movement.

Normally, the emblem is portrayed as a majestic, old-fashioned ship with all its sails open as it rides the ocean to a location unseen. Occasionally, some decks show a more modern ship, which can be coming to or leaving port.

This is an auspicious card that bodes well for your enterprises. The cards touching the Ship will describe opportunities, ones that you can use to further your goals and better your life. Traditionally, the Ship has been seen as business ventures, but even for non-entrepreneurs it brings an opportunity for betterment and enrichment.

Another meaning the Ship carries is that of inheritance. In practice, though, I've known it to be a gift or trust fund set up by someone else for you, which is set to mature or be paid out while the person who has done this is still alive.

When the Ship falls close to the querent's card, an opportunity for travel is to be expected. You should look carefully at the cards surrounding the Ship as the journey is usually important, but with bad cards it will be memorable for the wrong reasons.

Progressed Meanings:

When close to the querent's card the Ship is a card of travel, but it is distant travel – several hours, often more than the next county or state. The Ship can stand for the means of getting there: a train, a coach, an aeroplane, and of course, a boat.

A frequent meaning the Ship can add to the reading is that of longing for someone or something. Unlike the Anchor, which stands for hopes and desires, this longing may amount to no more than wishful thinking.

As the Ship also stands for inheritance, it is quite natural that it can show a death. Normally this is retrospective, and seen when the Ship follows several negative cards. It indicates missing that person, or bereavement.

For someone self-employed or involved in trade, the Ship is an important employment card.

Health: The Ship represents the liver, spleen, pancreas and gall bladder. It can also indicate sickness associated with travel, including fear of flying or sailing. In some cases it may show attachment disorders (Clouds + Stars + Ship).

4 – The House

King of Hearts

Keywords:
The home, private life, enterprise

The House's essence is that of sanctuary. Here, you can retreat into your personal domain and wait for better times, which it promises, or enjoy the fruits of your labours in times of plenty.

The Lenormand emblem is normally a 19th-century chateau set within a well-kept garden full of beautiful flowers and trees in full bloom. However, the ASS Lenormand shows a fabulous Art Deco residence.

This card symbolises your home and domestic affairs. A positive card, the House shows opportunities for improvement in your personal circumstances and prosperity. Good cards around the House bring you opportunities for happiness, and in some cases, chances to feather your nest and improve the quality of your life.

If difficult cards surround the House, but the House is close to your significator, you stand a stronger chance of overcoming troubles, even if your prospects appear bleak.

Should the House fall in the middle of the tableau it indicates a need for caution, particularly in domesticity or your neighbourhood. The cards around the House will elaborate the specifics. This is worsened if the significator card is directly above the House. The severity is increased if no cards separate the two vertically.

Progressed Meanings:

The House stands for your property, whether you live in a tower-block apartment, a country cottage or a river boat. Should there be enquiries about relocation, or the reading hints at it, the cards surrounding the House will describe where you're heading.

The House card shows the people you actually live with. This only includes your family if you share a roof.

This card also reveals your private life; it is the card of what goes on behind closed doors. House – Rod shows your private affairs will be talked about. When the House is near to the querent's card, it shows someone who likes to keep things grounded and private.

Like the Ship, the House can indicate business ventures. However, whereas the Ship describes opportunities, the House shows how these can better your standing and quality of life.

The King of Hearts can stand for a man. When the House describes a person he is either the same age as the querent, or more often, older. He will normally be in a comfortable position financially, friendly and family-orientated, but rarely related to the querent.

Health: The House represents the body as a whole. Nevertheless, it also signifies the skeleton and bones, as these are what hold you up. With the Mountain it can show osteoarthritis and calcification. In a reading for a sick person, this is one of the cards that is worth noting, particularly when free from bad cards, as it shows the body overall is strong enough and aided by good treatment. It is one of the cards that can offset the Tree.

5 – The Tree

7 of Hearts

Keywords:
Health, time, inertia

The essence of the Tree card is health.

A majority of Lenormand decks show an old, tall tree in bloom, either in a field or by a pathway. Sometimes the left side of the tree appears lusher, or the branches extend further when compared to the right side, which can betray signs of wilting.

The Tree represents your health. Whenever the Tree is near the significator, health will be of concern during the period covered by the reading.

Cards surrounding the Tree will always comment on your health and well-being, thus negative cards will need to be discerned with extra caution. When the Tree is far from the significator the severity of problems is reduced, but when it is close to the querent's card they are more severe.

When the Tree is close to the House, the Garden, the Paths or the Sun, some of the negativity around it is offset and recovery is foretold. This is especially auspicious when the Tree falls near the significator.

Progressed Meanings:

The Tree's primary meaning is that of your health. Health is not the same as sickness, so good cards around the Tree are promising in terms of a restoration to vitality, strength and good constitution. If this involves the House, the Garden, the Paths or the Sun you are very fortunate.

The Tree is a slow-paced card of lasting effect. If a 'when' question is asked, you are normally looking at a couple of years, if not longer. After all, trees do not grow overnight.

Because of this longevity, the Tree often symbolises a sense of inertia. If it falls between the significator and the partner card, it very often predicts a relationship continuing out of habit or convenience rather than being rooted in love.

Health: The Tree, in terms of health, talks about the general state of the body, how strong it is and the overall constitution. The cards around it indicate what is wrong and what is affecting your health; thus, negative cards become more severe.

6 – The Clouds

King of Clubs

Keywords:
Tribulation, problems, confusion

Misfortune is the essence of the Clouds.

Thick, dense clouds are the most common depiction of this card's emblem. Normally, one side will be shown as much darker than the other.

This is one of the most negative cards in the deck. Whatever touches the Clouds in a reading becomes troublesome and problematic. Its influence increases the closer it is to the significator card.

You should note which side it falls on in relation to the querent's card. To the left it heralds problems of shorter duration; to the right, difficulties of greater severity and length. Some decks show the darker side of the clouds on the right and you may, at personal discretion, reverse this rule.

Progressed Meanings:

The Clouds predicts problems that are not easily overcome. It can herald confusion and uncertainty, especially with cards denoting messages or answers. These can be difficult or upsetting due to being abstruse and unhelpful.

In any reading, we note the cards' proximity to the Clouds. Any card one position away from the Clouds takes its 'clouded*' meaning without fail. Cards vertically, and to a lesser extent diagonally, below the Clouds card become difficult, problematic and confusing. The severity is decided by whether the Clouds are to the left or right of the significator.

You should exercise caution with cards two positions away from the Clouds. Positive cards that are two positions away, but above the Clouds, will usually be affected far less than those below; this is because they are in the influencing position. However, should these be negative cards, you will normally find they will be clouded or at least function more malefic than normal.

Another meaning is bad weather of all varieties, often fog, storms, heavy winds and blizzards, which can obscure vision and make journeys hazardous. It also means pollution – not always air, with the Fish it can show polluted water.

As with the King of Clubs, the Clouds can describe a man, sometimes an ex-partner. The card the King looks at often shows where this man will trouble you. When it is describing someone it adds a sense of unpleasantness, a brusque manner, and can indicate grey or salt-and-pepper hair.

Health: The Clouds card is a symbol for the lungs and respiratory system, as well as airborne infections and seasonal illnesses (influenza).

* Please note only the Clouds can 'cloud' other cards. All negative cards can effect other cards, but they cannot *cloud* i.e. change other cards' meanings.

7 – The Snake

Queen of Clubs

Keywords:
Treachery, complications, twists and turns

The Snake's essence is sedition in that she brings trouble and complications.

Depending on the deck, the Snake can be shown coiled around a tree stump or poised to attack like a viper. No. 194115 Mlle Lenormand, published by Piatnik, shows a cobra.

The Snake, when it's far away from your card and the Clouds, indicates that problems should soon be solved and your current difficulties will lessen. If it is close, it warns you to be on your guard. Treachery, often in your friendships and relationships, will soon reveal itself. The cards touching the Snake should be carefully examined as they will reveal the source of the treachery and you can then take steps to safeguard against it.

Progressed Meanings:

The Snake is certainly not a nice card, but it is not an evil card. I am often asked what the difference between the Snake and the Fox is. If the Snake hurts you then she does so on a personal level: she will take your partner or betray you as a friend. Whereas the Fox always takes something more tangible, such as your clientele and livelihood, or he will defraud you.

This card has a bad habit of turning up in matters of love. It's never a good sign to see the Snake near the Heart, as it brings complicated and often upsetting developments. With other cards of bad omen, the Snake can herald unfaithfulness.

Careful attention should be paid when this card is with the Fox. When the Snake precedes the Fox it shows an intelligent woman, one you may not like, but who is, fortunately, trustworthy. If the Snake follows the Fox then she is someone untrustworthy.

The Snake can stand for a woman. Describing a person, she is normally intelligent, but not easily likeable.

This card is also a symbol for rivers, brooks, streams and inland water. With the Paths card it can show winding pathways, roads or country lanes.

The Snake is the female same-sex partner card.

Health: This card represents the intestines, particularly the large bowel and down into the rectum. It also adds a sense of complication and uncertainty to health problems.

8 – The Coffin

9 of Diamonds

Keywords:
Sickness, endings, losses

The Coffin symbolises the essence of loss.

Normally, we see a Coffin, sometimes on a bier and partially covered with a pall. The Mystical Lenormand shows an Egyptian sarcophagus.

A thoroughly unpleasant and negative card, the Coffin predicts sickness and lasting losses, which are often financial and crippling when it is close the querent's card. The severity of this is increased by the attendance of another malefic card. The Coffin's presence diminishes good cards, too.

When it falls far away the severity is reduced, but it still brings bleak times, endings and illness of a shorter duration. At best, these troubles can be transitory or minor, and you may stand a chance of recouping finances with considerable effort.

Progressed Meanings:

The Coffin is about endings, not about transformations. Don't confuse the two. Whatever falls immediately before the Coffin is set to end, and often the card that follows it is somewhat diminished or becomes sickly.

Principally a card of sickness, the Coffin shows the debilitating effects of illness. It is often said to be a diagnosed ailment. When the Coffin is close to the Tree, the card of health, or the Tower, the card of life and longevity, you should pay careful attention. You could be seeing a negative and lasting effect on the querent's health.

If the card describes a person, he or she is normally sickly or depressed. This is particularly true when the Coffin precedes the person card. If the Coffin is to the right, the person may be extremely musical, or reclusive.

The Coffin can show being boxed in, and in a question of 'where' it can indicate boxes, bureaus, closets and cupboards.

Health: The Coffin is the card of sickness. Very often this is debilitating and chronic. It could indicate depression, or something that causes depression. In daily draws the Coffin often predicts a severe headache.

9 – The Bouquet

Queen of Spades

Keywords:
Happiness, assistance, gifts

Happiness is the essence of the Bouquet.

Our most common representation of this emblem is a simple small bouquet or vase of various bright coloured flowers.

One of the most positive cards in the pack, the Bouquet is a card of happiness and joy, especially in your day-to-day affairs. It symbolises companionship and the simple pleasures of life. With good cards, you might even get a nice surprise.

Even when it falls far away, unless it is surrounded by very negative cards, the Bouquet promises that the querent will have people who support him, or at least offer comfort in times of difficulty, even if they are not in a position to help him.

Progressed Meanings:

There is an 'old world' flavour to the Bouquet card. Qualities of good manners, consideration and even being kempt all fall under the Bouquet, whether it is indicating a need for the querent to pay attention to these features or describing a person.

Traditionally, when it falls with the Ring a proposal follows. This can be an offer of marriage, you could be asked out on a date, or a friend might ask you to lunch. Context does matter.

This card symbolises flowers of all varieties, including lilies, as card 30, the Lily, never symbolises real flowers. It also represents insects.

The Bouquet can stand for a woman. When the querent has several grandchildren, the Bouquet can be her adult daughters and the Child her grandchildren.

Health: The Bouquet promises recovery and points to complementary and homeopathic remedies as an aid. With negative cards it can indicate allergies.

10 – The Scythe

Jack of Diamonds

Keywords:
Danger, aggression, criminality

This card's essence is danger.

On this card, we normally see a traditional scythe with its sharpened blade and handle. Depending on the deck, it can point right or left.

The Scythe is a warning to be on guard. It's a sign that you are in danger of severe loss or injury. Cards touching the Scythe need to be examined carefully to understand where the threat is looming.

If the Scythe is far away from the significator the danger or aggression is often directed towards the querent's associates. When close to the querent's card, the Scythe diminishes the effect of any good cards that surround it.

Progressed Meanings:

The card that follows the Scythe normally represents what is under threat, or describes the danger. When the Scythe strikes it cuts away something, be it a relationship, your job, your home, et cetera, and the loss is unequivocal.

If a person card precedes the Scythe, that individual may appear very suddenly. However, it more often describes the person as being overbearing, if not outright aggressive or intimidating. A need for caution is advised.

The Scythe also stands for criminality. It can indicate an assault or a crime that puts you in danger.

The Scythe is a symbol of all things sharp, such as a knife, a needle or a razor blade. It's also the card of weapons, including guns.

Health: The Scythe can indicate fractures, torn ligaments, injuries through crime, and with the Cavalier it may foretell a car crash. It also symbolises surgery and injections.

11 – The Rod

Jack of Clubs

Keywords:
Strife, discussions, twice

The essence of the Rod is discord.

This card is variously called the Rod, Whips or Broom. In most decks, the Rod is shown not as a bullwhip or cat-o-nine tail, but as a bundle of birch rod (a bundle of birch twigs), historically used to beat children or for judicial punishment. Some decks show both a birch rod and a whip while others show a broom.

The Rod is not a nice card. It forecasts anything from the coming of tension to outright strife and animosity to the querent's personal life, family and close friends. The severity is judged by the Rod's proximity to the querent's card. The root of the unrest is often described by the cards immediately touching the Rod.

Extra care should be paid to the Rod when it's in the vicinity of the Tree, the Coffin or the Tower because the querent could suffer a sudden period of ill health or a relapse.

Progressed Meanings:

Often the Rod is a card of face-to-face communications; however, these are normally on the heated side and the advice is to choose your words well and not inflame situations.

Strife augured by this card is most often within relationships, family or friendships. For this reason, careful attention must be paid when the Rod falls with the House. Before the House card, it often indicates strife in the home; if the Rod follows the House, your personal life might be the topic of gossip.

When the Rod is in attendance with the Ring you need to be careful. Depending on context this can indicate difficulties and disputes in a relationship, or in official or contractual discussions.

The Rod is derived from the ancient Roman fasces. For this reason it also stands for legal documents, writing, official debates, trials, trade unions and summonses. With the Letter it can be a summons or service of notice.

It's one of several cards to denote two of something. With the Rod this is often an indicator of repetition; a test might need to be taken twice, a document redrafted, a sickness returns. But please note, it means you will do it twice but not endless repetition (which is the Ring).

Health: The Rod indicates the throat and voice. However, it's also a symbol of recurring ailments and relapses and is particular worrying when with cards of health.

12 – The Birds

7 of Diamonds

Keywords:
Upsets, stress, announcements

Upsets are the essence of the Birds card.

On this deck, we normally see two small birds, either sitting in a tree on branches or around a nest. The well-known Blaue Eule pattern, published by Königsfurt-Urania, calls this card the Owls and shows two owls in a tree on what appears to be a foggy night. Whether the card is known as the Birds or the Owls, the meaning remains the same.

The Birds stands for upsets and stresses when it falls close to the significator. These troubles tend to be related to a disappointment, or to work-related stress the querent cannot do much about. The cards nearby will elaborate the specifics. The good news is that the problems will soon pass unless the card is with the Clouds.

When the Birds is located at a distance from the querent's card it predicts that a sudden journey will take place. This is usually a happy surprise.

Progressed Meanings:

When the Birds follows the Child card, it predicts that a pregnancy will be learned about during the period covered by the reading. This does not necessarily have to be for the querent.

These days the Birds often plays out in one of two ways: It either indicates stresses in everyday life or conversations and gossip. The latter is very true in daily draws or readings covering just a few weeks' time.

The Birds can stand for two people, such as an aunt and uncle. It can also indicate double or two of something, such as double the luck (with the Clover or the Sun) or two lots of money. When the Birds is describing a person, with negative cards they can be sorrowful and stressed, otherwise they are often talkative and indiscreet (think 'sing like a canary').

It's also the card of small domestic and wild birds up to the size of owls.

Health: The Birds represents the eyes. It is a sign of anxiety disorders when with the Clouds, and palpitations or blood pressure problems when with the Heart.

13 – The Child

Jack of Spades

Keywords:
Trust, little, children

The Child is the essence of simplicity.

Normally, the Child card's emblem is a small, prepubescent girl, or occasionally a boy. The child can be shown holding a posy or playing with a toy.

The Child shows how your friends and loved ones see you. When the Child falls close to the significator card, you are assured of the respect and assistance of your associates. When the Child falls farther away it indicates trust, but friends may not be in a position to help you should negative cards be around the Child or the significator.

Progressed Meanings:

Naturally, the Child card will represent the querent's children or grandchildren. When it's attended by the Birds it indicates either a pregnancy or news (often anxious in nature) about a pregnancy or child. For this reason, careful attention should be paid to the cards around the Child in terms of problems or issues.

There is a naiveté about a person described by the Child card. She can be innocent, overly trusting, or unprepared for some of the issues of everyday life. However, she is normally very kind and helpful.

The 'little' can be literal. A person might be short in stature or younger than the querent. When the Child follows the Fish it can indicate a little money. Depending on context this can mean that the querent is poor – he only has that little bit.

Health: This card indicates traditional childhood illnesses and ailments such as chicken pox, growing pains or whooping cough.

14 – The Fox

9 of Clubs

Keywords:
Deceit, wrong, fraud

Wrongness is the essence of the Fox card.

Normally, the Fox emblem shows a lone, predatory fox that sometimes has a fowl in its mouth or appears set to pounce. The Brepols pattern, currently published by Carta Mundi as Jeu Lenormand, shows a fox taking a goose home to its family.

The Fox symbolises that something is wrong in the querent's life and that he needs to take care. Whilst the cards surrounding the Fox will give you the specifics, theft and fraud are frequently augured by this card. Normally this is perpetrated by someone known to the querent.

If the Fox is far away and free of bad cards, it indicates that you might be judging someone unfairly and that you do not need to be so cautious.

Progressed Meanings:

Primarily, the Fox's keyword is 'wrong'.

The card that falls after it is worth close attention as it shows something that should not be taken at face value. This also applies to people cards immediately following the Fox.

The Fox points towards cheats and thefts, rarely petty, and it can indicate professional sabotage. This tends to be related to rivalry in the workplace, someone you are in competition with. Alone, however, the Fox has nothing to do with work save commenting on someone's work ethic or lack of one.

Marie Marco's wonderful book was the first published that specifically associated the Fox with salaried employment. All French and French-derived books published since have mostly followed this pattern. This appears to be derived from a revisionist view of the Renert fables, popular in Belgium, France and Luxembourg. Since the late 19th century, Renert has been viewed less as a con artist and trickster and more as the working man's hero, helping oppressed workers. This reached its zenith with the anti-Semitic *Van den vos Reynaerde* by Robert van Genechten. In addition, Marco's book organised the cards by their pips. It is also possible that she was influenced by misidentifying the German acorns as French tréfles (clover). Regardless, if the Fox as 'work' is your preferred association that is okay. Many of my students elect to use the Fox. Go with what works for you. But for me, it is too far removed from its other traditional associations and how the card works in readings.

In certain contexts the Fox can say your approach, or idea, is wrong. Thus it counsels caution. This is usually only when you are asking if you would be right to do something, and so on. Context is important.

If the Fox touches cards of health it can indicate a misdiagnosis, and a second opinion may be advisable.

The Fox represents actual foxes. It's also the card of cats.

Health: The Fox symbolises the nose. It can also indicate a need for caution, as something might be masked by another problem, or a diagnosis or treatment may need to be reviewed. Tread carefully.

15 – The Bear

10 of Clubs

Keywords:
Power, protection, envy

The Bear's essence is power. Power is good only for those who have it, but it also brings enemies and breeds envy.

Most decks show one large Eurasian brown bear, now most commonly found in Eastern Europe but previously common in parts of Germany, where the oracle appeared. The bear on the card can be shown hunting for food or resting. Ciro Marchetti's Gilded Reverie Lenormand has a gorgeous polar bear.

The Bear is a dichotomy: on one hand it promises you good fortune and prosperity, and in times of difficulty, the protection of strong allies; but it also warns you against those who might abuse or resent your good luck.

When bad cards surround the Bear, or it falls far away from the significator, it is wise to trust only those you are closest to and watch for those who might benefit from your misfortune. You may soon discover that those you saw as allies are those who plot against you.

Progressed Meanings:

The Bear often stands for a person – usually a woman – who holds some influence over you. Most of the time this will be your mother, grandmother, an aunt, et cetera. Unless bad cards are around the Bear you can rely on this woman for aid, comfort and support.

In the context of work, the Bear represents the person you report to, your immediate supervisor, line manager or team leader.

A person described by the Bear is usually imposing and strong, either physically or mentally.

The Bear indicates good luck in financial dealings. Since money is a form of power, the Bear is a good gauge of where you currently stand in terms of individual prosperity. It's worth remembering this isn't so much about your salary, but rather how you're doing with savings, pension plans, health insurance, et cetera. It's how your money is working for you.

This card can indeed show a real bear, or other large wild animal, but this isn't something that will come up too often!

Health: Anatomically, the Bear stands for the stomach and eating habits. It's also the card that symbolises hair.

16 – The Stars

6 of Hearts

Keywords:
Success, night, north

The essence of the Stars is good luck.

The traditional emblem for this card is a clear night sky full of several twinkling stars. Below, there is sometimes a landscape scene.

The Stars promises success in your endeavours and any projects undertaken during the period covered by the reading. The cards that touch the Stars should prove successful and lucky when this card is especially close to (and preferably above) the significator. The card's luck wanes when it's far away.

If the Stars falls with negative cards, or the Clouds is close to the significator, it warns you of long stretches of bad luck and problems in your projects that you did not anticipate.

Progressed Meanings:

My Grandfather had a saying that would be translated as, 'Never make camp under a starless sky.' For this reason, I see the Stars as a card of guidance that tells me where best to concentrate my efforts – where to make camp. The area normally brings benefits, often tangible but also emotional, that are right for me at that time. So, if it is surrounded by cards of work, then this should be where I focus my attentions; alternatively, if the cards of family surround the Stars, I will know it's time to prioritise my kin.

In certain contexts, the Stars can indicate both science and fortune-telling, though the former is more common. When it falls after a person card, it could show a scientist or a person who has a good head for figures, just as much as it might denote an astrologer, medium or card reader.

The Stars can indicate the human mind as a whole. It can reflect how happy and clear-sighted you are. With negative cards, you may be prone to bad judgements and depression.

In terms of timing, the Stars stands for night. It is also traditionally seen as the north.

Health: The Stars represents the skin. It can also indicate problems with the brain's functioning as well as issues involving sleep.

17 – The Storks

Queen of Hearts

Keywords:
Changes, relocation, birth

The Storks' essence is change, particularly in relation to your domestic life, whether a new home, the arrival of a new addition to the family or just a change in outlook.

Lenormand cards show the European migratory white stork species. Some packs' emblem is one stork standing in water, its leg poised to move, while others show two – one in flight and one nesting – emphasising the change and endings associated with this bird and this card.

When the Storks falls very close to the querent's card it augurs changes and improvements. Traditionally, it forecasts relocation to a new address, but these days it might just mean home improvements.

Should the card fall far away or with especially negative cards, the querent's situation is static and set to remain the same for some time. Depending on the influence of the cards surrounding the Storks this can lead to upsets and frustrations.

Progressed Meanings:

Primarily, the Storks talks about a change which, free of bad cards, will be towards something better – an improvement in a situation, progress to the next stage, even a promotion at work.

Whilst the Moon is the primary card dealing with honour, the Storks can bring an opportunity for recognition to the area denoted by the card below it. When the Storks crowns the significator or key cards the querent can expect a time of promotion or elevation.

When the Storks follows the Child it can indicate the forthcoming birth of a child, however, this is never unexpected news to the querent. A pregnancy yet unrevealed is shown by the Birds following the Child, not the Storks.

With the Tower, the Storks shows major life changes. Occasionally, with the addition of the Ship, a bereavement is forecast. Remember, the white stork was for centuries associated with death.

The Storks can stand for a woman. When it describes someone, she can be tall, ambitious or even a restless soul, and often someone working in the travel sector.

Health: The Storks is a card of improvement and upturn in health problems. It also stands for the legs and mobility in general.

18 – The Dog

10 of Hearts

Keywords:
Friendship, trustworthiness, a man

Loyalty is the essence the Dog brings. This card speaks of faithful friendships that can aid you in your time of need and someone to watch your back.

Most decks show the dog in its master's garden either standing or lying in front of a kennel with its ears piqued, ready to warn or greet you. A working guard dog!

When the Dog is close to the querent's card it promises good, faithful and lasting friendships and alliances. If it falls far away, the querent might experience some disappointment in his friendships, and those he relies on might prove less steadfast.

When surrounded by the Clouds, or other negative cards, the Dog is a warning not to readily trust those you are unsure of. Friendships can be broken or tested, and those you trust might turn out to be disloyal.

Progressed Meanings:

The Dog can stand for any friend in the querent's life, but it is also a card that can represent a man, sometimes this can be an ex-partner. When it describes a person, he is invariably known to the querent as friendly, loyal and trustworthy.

Man has long worked alongside and with dogs. If the Fox is our work rivals, the Dog is our work allies. Your colleagues of either gender will appear as the Dog. Should you supervise or employ people, the Dog will describe these individuals. Thus should you be considering hiring someone, the cards around the Dog will describe both their work standards and trustworthiness.

The Dog can represent our pets in general, but it is specifically the card of dogs.

Health: The Dog stands for a carer – be it a doctor, nurse or other health worker. Anatomically it represents the mouth, tongue and teeth.

19 – The 'High' Tower

6 of Spades

Keywords:
Age, official, isolation

The Tower is a symbol of the essence of longevity.

Normally, on this card we see the emblem of a high tower from which people would have looked out and surveyed their surroundings. Sometimes, we see a few crumbling battlements, which imply that only the tower is left.

The Tower is a card of longevity and old age. Surrounded by good cards it promises you a happy, healthy and long retirement, with security and protection in your old age. Thus, this card should always be examined in connection with the Tree and the Coffin.

When the Tower falls with negative cards – especially the Clouds or the Coffin – you should take extra care of your health. Recurring sickness, a relapse or health conditions that are debilitating or chronic are all possible.

Progressed Meanings:

This card can indicate periods of solitary life. This is especially true when the Tower falls between the querent's card and the partner card, which can indicate a schism, even divorce, normally instigated by the person to the Tower's left. Near to the Heart, or just to the right of a person card, it indicates a period of loneliness through separation, divorce or widowhood.

The Tower can stand for buildings of high importance: a courthouse, government building, tax office or university. Combined with cards of money or employment it can indicate long-term goals, even pension plans.

This card can represent a man, frequently the querent's father, grandfather, uncle and so on. When it precedes a person card it describes the person as ambitious, aloof or of some official importance.

Traditionally, the card was a card of happiness. I have this as true, however, it is a solipsistic happiness; you may be made happy by the Tower, but other people do not benefit.

Health: The card stands for longevity. It can indicate strong health or long-lasting problems, depending on the proportion of positive or negative cards nearby. Anatomically, the Tower stands for the spine.

20 – The 'Forest' Garden

8 of Spades

Keywords:
Community, public, society

The Garden is the essence of interaction.

Predominantly, this card's emblem is a beautiful, serene public space. Before the early 20th century, parks were often most people's only access to green spaces in large cities such as Berlin or Paris and where people would meet to socialise or even ride in their coaches if they were wealthy. A few decks show a more private place, such as a large house's garden.

When the Garden falls far away from the significator or is under the influence of negative cards, the querent should beware false friends and expect periods of loneliness and isolation. A period of rejection often ensues.

Close to the significator, the Garden promises new friendships and alliances which can lead to a fruitful improvement in the querent's affairs. Close to the Dog or the Tower, these connections and improvements will prove lasting and the querent may soon have her personal status increased.

Progressed Meanings:

The Garden stands for the public and society in general. It frequently appears as a public space, including places of history or heritage, hospitals, restaurants and the theatre, as well as actual parks and woodlands.

In attendance with the Cavalier, the Letter or the Rod it denotes public notices or debates; however, with the Letter it can be social networking sites such as Facebook or other Internet forums.

When it describes a person, it's important to note card order. Before a person card, it describes a socialite, someone who is friends with everyone – a traditional social butterfly. When the Garden follows a person card, it describes a 'queen bee' who is very selective of her circle.

Health: The Garden denotes a hospital or a place of treatment, such as a convalescent home. In some cases it describes contagion and an illness spread by contact with people.

21 – The Mountain

8 of Clubs

Keywords:
Blockage, enemy, barrier

The Mountain card is the essence of obstacles.

Most Lenormand packs depict the Mountain card using a high and rocky peak or a distant mountain in a wintery landscape; it is always a remote and unforgiving terrain with a cold atmosphere.

When the Mountain falls far away from the querent's card it denotes a powerful ally who can aid the querent in times of difficulty, especially if the Dog and the Garden are near the significator.

However, when the Mountain is located close to the significator it indicates that the querent has a rival or opponent who will hinder or attack at the earliest opportunity. Expect blockages and problems. The severity or power of the foe and hindrances is based on the Mountain's proximity to the querent's card, and is worsened by the attendance of negative cards.

Progressed Meanings:

Frequently, the Mountain will either manifest as a barrier to a goal or aspiration or as an actual enemy. The latter should not be dismissed as a fallacy left over from an uneducated age. Enemies exist. Depending on context this can be anything from your rival at work, to a bully, to cigarettes when you are trying to quit smoking.

As a blockage or an enemy the Mountain is not insurmountable, but the challenge to climb it is often doubtful and lengthy, with no promise of successful overcoming.

The Mountain can also indicate another country, especially one you share a border with, as well as someone from another country.

Health: Often the Mountain indicates calcification, sclerosis (hardening) or stenosis (narrowing), or a blockage in a particular part of the body's functioning. It also represents the skull in anatomy.

22 – The Paths

Queen of Diamonds

Keywords:
Choices, intersection, crises

The essence of the Paths card is choice.

A crossroads, often with no signpost or indication of destination, is the most common depiction of this card's emblem. Depending on the individual deck, the emblem can show green pastures in the distance and two or three intersecting paths.

If the Paths card falls far away from the significator and is free of negative cards, it indicates that problems can and will be overcome, but the querent will need to use initiative.

Should the Paths fall by the Clouds, then the card always denotes a crisis, very often involving upheaval and painful choices. This is made worse the nearer the Clouds and the Paths fall to the significator.

Free from negative influence, and near to the querent's card, the Paths indicates that anxious times will soon present themselves. A problem or important intersection on the querent's life journey will manifest; however, the worries will pass when a decision is made. The cards around the Paths will hint at what the decision relates to.

Progressed Meanings:

Most of the time, the Paths indicates that the querent has options and choices in the area being enquired about. Whilst this is not always the result of a crisis or negative situation, seeing this card is a clear indication of the need for careful discernment. Once a choice is made the Paths often indicates that it will be hard to turn back should you change your mind.

Near the Clouds this card is particularly malefic as it indicates several problems converging. Should the Coffin, the Scythe or the Mountain also be near, this is magnified. The choice – if one still has one – is painful and often heart-wrenching, and problems and upset of long duration are frequently the order of the day.

The Paths can be a literal road. For this reason, it can indicate regular journeys, travel to the next town, commutes and work-related travel. Should you see the Scythe or the Snake nearby in this context, you should beware your travel arrangements.

This card can stand for a woman.

Health: The Paths is one of the cards that can mitigate the Tree, indicating that treatment and solutions will be found. Therefore, medically, it's a sign that options should be carefully explored. Anatomically, the Paths relates to the arteries and veins.

23 – The Mice

7 of Clubs

Keywords:
Theft, loss, anxieties

The Mice carries the essence of erosion.

A majority of decks show at least two small mice around food – such as cheese or bread – which they are quickly devouring while the house owner is away. Occasionally, a rat replaces the mice.

The Mice symbolises a loss, sometimes through theft, but also through carelessness on the part of the querent, which can be recovered should the Mice fall close to the querent's card. Should the Mice be located at a distance, this loss is seldom recouped.

Progressed Meanings:

In a reading you should note the cards to either side of the Mice, for they both bring a loss. The card to the left of the Mice is what is set to be soiled or destroyed, and the card to the right of the Mice is what that will cause you to lose or lose out on. Don't be lulled into a false sense of security if the cards flanking the Mice are negative, as you will still lose out in some shape or form.

The Mice close to the significator points to some anxiety for the querent. Unlike the Birds, this is not normally short-lived and may indicate a lasting dispiritedness and even passive-aggressive tendencies. For this reason, when describing someone, the person can either be somewhat 'rat-faced', or simply passive-aggressive or draining.

The Mice can stand for real mice, but also rats, hamsters, guinea pigs, rabbits and other small rodents, both domestic and wild.

Health: This card is very difficult in health matters because it can present in several ways. Anatomically, the Mice can be an ulcer, necrotic tissue, a tumour or even parasites (as these things 'eat' at the body), but it can also indicate stress and panic-related disorders – especially things like alopecia.

24 – The Heart

Jack of Hearts

Keywords:
Love, affection, warmth

Affection is the essence of the Heart card. What tugs at your heartstrings – be it a cause, a dear relative or the amorous stirrings of romance – is all symbolised by this card.

In most decks, the emblem is an ideographic heart sometimes surrounded by roses and stems which often have at least one ominous thorn.

If free from negative cards, the Heart promises happiness and love. Should this card fall very near the querent's card then romantic relationships – new or old – will almost certainly be a feature of her future, the seriousness of which is revealed by the proximity of the Ring and the Anchor.

Progressed Meanings:

The Heart's main meaning is love, of which, naturally, romantic love will be a strong feature. When the Heart is near the querent's card, his romantic life will come under the spotlight. New love is around the corner, or an existing relationship becomes more serious or, if it was flagging, improves. Check what is touching the Heart for details. Note that you need the Ring and the Anchor to be in favourable positions for this to be lasting.

When the Heart is far away, it can show platonic love or simply strong friendships, but should the Clouds fall near the Heart or the significator, then deep disappointment is the Heart's prediction. Similarly, the Coffin, the Scythe, the Mountain or the Cross near the Heart all augur pain. Should the Snake or the Fox be near the Heart then complicated and difficult, or simply the wrong love, respectively, is the meaning.

Love doesn't always need to be romantic. Near the cards of home, friendship, work or money, the Heart signifies a sense of love and happiness in these respective areas.

Health: The Heart symbolises the heart itself, but also the cardiopulmonary and circulatory systems in general. Near the Birds, it is a sign of high blood pressure or palpitations.

25 – The Ring

Ace of Clubs

Keywords:
Marriage, contract, connections

The essence of the Ring card is ties.

Most Lenormand decks show a simple but elegant woman's engagement ring with a precious stone or two. The ASS Lenormand includes a presentation box.

The Ring's meaning is determined by which side of the querent's card it falls on. To the left of the significator, it augurs the possibility of a separation that is more severe or inevitable the farther away the Ring is. To the right of the querent's card it indicates a lasting relationship, or a new one, that is stronger the closer the Ring is.

Progressed Meanings:

The Ring frequently appears in terms of romantic relationships. Seeing it to the right of the querent's card and close by is a strong sign that his relationship will be lasting or that a new – and serious – love is around the corner. Should the Ring be to the left of the querent's card, note how far away it is and what the Heart and the Anchor are doing before predicting it is all over. Should the Anchor be near the significator, and not touched by negative cards, then both parties are willing to try.

Another meaning of the Ring is contracts of all kinds. Frequently this will mean employment, but it can also be a mortgage or house lease. If the Coffin, the Scythe or the Cross falls with the Anchor these important connections will be sorely tested, if not severed.

Health: The Ring stands for illnesses which can be both progressive and debilitating, and sadly, sometimes incurable or chronic. It also frequently indicates co-morbidity, whereby two illnesses exist simultaneously; they do not arise one out of the other, but can exacerbate, or sometimes mask, each other.

26 – The Book

10 of Diamonds

Keywords:
Secrets, education, the unknown

The Book represents the essence of the unknown. The original name for this card was Grimoire.

Normally, we see this card's emblem as either a closed or open leather-bound book sitting on a table. One deck shows part of the book in shadow, and there is seldom a title to be seen.

When the Book falls near the significator it indicates that something important, and frequently upsetting, will be revealed to the querent. When it is far away it indicates a secret that is more surprising than upsetting. Should bad cards touch the Book it is deeply negative wherever it is dealt.

Progressed Meanings:

The Book often simply means that the querent doesn't know something. Thus, she needs to do her research or sit and wait for events to unfold; acting prematurely might jeopardise her chances or lead to upset.

The 'unknown' nature of the Book means it frequently appears as education. Should the querent be job-searching, he might need to brush up his qualifications. If he is asking about returning to school, look to see if good cards touch the Book – that's a green light.

When the Book falls before a person card it normally indicates you do not yet know that person; falling after, it might describe someone educated or bookish.

The Rod is the main writer card. However, the Book can stand for real books and for a writer, as it represents his published material.

Health: The Book represents the brain and cognition. Depending on where it falls this can be impaired function (Mountain), olfactory bulb (Fox) or brain trauma (Scythe). It can also stand for undiagnosed medical problems.

27 – The Letter

7 of Spades

Keywords:
Telephone calls, paper, superficiality

The Letter symbolises the essence of communication.

Most Lenormand decks portray the Letter as an unopened envelope or sometimes as a calling card or small note on a message tray.

Wherever the Letter falls it denotes the arrival of news, rarely in person. The nature of the news is revealed by the cards with it.

When the Clouds is near the querent's card, or near the Letter itself, the news will be something unpleasant that requires your attention.

Progressed Meanings:

Unlike the Cavalier, the news predicted from the Letter is seldom delivered in person – although when the two cards fall together, you can expect couriered parcels or documents. It is the card of communication that occurs without being face-to-face. Thus it augurs telephone calls, SMS, emails and, of course, letters. As a simple rule, when the Letter falls to the right of a person card, or ends a row, the querent can expect to receive the telephone call, letter, et cetera. When the Letter comes first, the querent makes the call.

The Letter takes much of its significance from the cards it is with. Positive cards indicate that you can expect news or replies, negative cards indicate bad news. Context counts. The Coffin with the Letter can be a rejection letter, not just news of a death. If the Clouds is involved, the Letter is a harbinger of significant problems.

The Letter stands for all paper and card items, including your fortune-telling cards.

When the Letter precedes a person card it means the person is superficial. Similarly, before the Heart, the Lily or the Anchor, it adds a fleeting quality to love, sex and happiness, or stability, respectively.

Health: The Letter can stand for letters from a doctor, and also for pamphlets and prescriptions. Anatomically, it stands for fingers.

28 – The Lord

Ace of Hearts

Keywords:
Man, male querent, significator card

The Lord card personifies the masculine essence and will, thus, always stand for a male person.

On the card, the Lord is typically shown as a tall and well-dressed man in the prime of his life and is frequently depicted purposefully gazing right, as if waiting for someone. The Gilded Reverie Lenormand portrays the Lord looking left.

The Lord represents the male querent.

If the querent is female, the Lord denotes the most important man in her life. This can be her partner, male friend, boss, brother or sometimes her father.

Progressed Meanings:

When the Lord isn't the significator it will frequently represent the querent's love interest. Should the querent be a lesbian, the Snake will show her partner. Nevertheless, the Lord will still be someone in her life – from her brother to her father, or a friend.

If the querent is a gay man, his partner card is the Cavalier.

29 – The Lady

Ace of Spades

Keywords:
Woman, female querent, significator card

The Lady is the embodiment of the female essence and, thus, always represents a woman.

On this card, we always see a female figure. She is normally youthful, well-dressed, elegant and shown in profile. Typically, she is shown looking left, but decks such as the Dondorf and Brepols patterns show her looking right.

The Lady represents the female querent.

If the querent is male, the Lady stands for the most important woman in his life. This can be his partner, female friend, sister, boss or sometimes his mother.

Progressed Meanings:

When the Lady isn't the significator it will often represent the querent's love interest. Should the querent be homosexual, the Lady will still be someone in his life such as a sister or female friend.

If the querent is a lesbian, her partner card is the Snake.

30 – The Lily

King of Spades

Keywords:
Euphoria, sexuality, protection

The essence of the Lily card is ecstasy.

Most Petit Lenormand decks show a branch or bouquet of several Madonna lilies native to the Balkans. While most historians believe the fleur-de-lis was actually an iris rather than a lily, the lily symbol has become synonymous with several royal families of Europe and the monarchy's duties to protect, nurture and endure, and emphasises masculine values.

When the Lily card falls below the querent's card it indicates that she is set for a difficult time and unhappiness, and that her overall character will be sorrowful. Should the Lily fall above the significator it predicts happiness and a character most virtuous.

Progressed Meanings:

The main meaning of the Lily is that of your family in general, but especially your children, siblings and cousins. It can be the seeker's adult male offspring, when the Child is their grandchildren. If you live alone look to the Lily, not to the House, for what your family's fortune is. Favourable cards around the Lily predict that your family will be blessed with happiness and joy, and also stand steadfast with you.

Good cards around the Lily and the Lily falling above your significator are always a strong sign of happiness. Unlike the Bouquet this is a deeper or more enduring happiness.

As the card deals with your offspring, it also deals with your sex life. With the Sun, it indicates sexual pleasure and sated desires, but, as context matters, it can just show a happy family. Should the Scythe fall before the Lily it can be a sign of deviancy and sexual harassment or rape.

In some circumstances, the Lily is a sign of official protection by agencies that have a duty to provide care and aid, such as social and health care organisations.

Health: The Lily stands for all sexual health. Anatomically, however, it represents the male sexual organs.

31 – The Sun

Ace of Diamonds

Keywords:
Success, good fortune, optimism

The Sun symbolises the essence of success.

On this card, we see a brilliant, vibrant sun shining in the sky. Sometimes, there are a few clouds or hints of the preceding night, which the sun's rays seem to vanquish.

If the Sun falls far away from the querent's card it shows despondency and difficulties that, frequently, the querent will not have the courage to face. Should the Clouds fall by the Sun it shows a reversal of fortune and severe bad luck.

However, with the Sun near the significator and free of bad cards, the querent should expect good luck, successful ventures and fortitude in all his dealings.

Progressed Meanings:

The Sun stands for big luck (to the Clover's little luck). Successful overcoming, improvement in all affairs, new starts and happiness can be delivered by this card. If the Birds follows the Sun, your luck is doubled.

The Sun, when it's far away from the querent's card, shows that the querent will have to expend much effort to overcome whatever trials he is facing. Frequently this proves too much, and thus can show a loss of mettle. When the Sun describes someone, he is charming, sunny and full of optimism; this reverses with bad cards.

Another meaning of the Sun is electricity, so it's worth exercising caution when it's by cards of warning.

Health: The main meaning of the Sun is energy and vitality. When this is impaired you become lethargic and spent. It can also denote drying out, thus dehydration, or with the Stars, dry skin.

32 – The Moon

8 of Hearts

Keywords:
Work, honours, fame

Adulation is the essence of the Moon card.

Predominately, the Moon card is shown as a peaceful landscape, normally at dusk, which is dominated by a crescent, waxing moon.

If the Moon falls close to the querent's card it promises that she will be recognised and met with honours and acclaim, even fame. You can expect adulation and accolades from the Moon, the sort which frequently bring tangible benefits.

However, should the Moon fall with negative cards or far away from the querent's card, it shows that she will be passed over and enter a fallow period that frequently brings misery.

Progressed Meanings:

Most people become famous and receive their fortunes and any honours through their careers. For this reason, the Moon principally talks about your profession and how well it's going. Good cards around the Moon show that you can expect a good spell at work and that it's a good time to try for that promotion or pay rise. Whilst the Anchor brings stability in employment, it relies on the Moon card being favourable if you want to be promoted, or to get and keep the job.

If you are job-searching, the Moon talks about the strength of your CV and how you perform in interviews. You need to impress and stand out (fame) to be selected (honour).

The Moon is a positive card for tangible rewards from your professional life, too. The Fish by the Moon will bring a good bonus or raise, and the Cavalier can be a company car. All status symbols come through this card.

It is a validation card and makes you 'feel good'.

When it describes someone, you should not dismiss the fame aspect. It does happen, but it can also mean someone with a legendary personality, classical good looks or somebody who looks like someone famous.

Health: In anatomy, the Moon stands for the female reproductive system. However, in general it reflects your self-esteem and how you feel about yourself. With bad cards, it can show body dysmorphia and self-loathing or depression.

33 – The Key

8 of Diamonds

Keywords:
Yes, certainty, providence

The Key's essence is providence.

Our most common representation for this card is a simple, old-fashioned key. Often it has a large bit section.

When the Key falls very close to the querent's card, it's a sign that ventures will go well and aspirations are within reach. The querent will need to work for what he wants, but providence is on his side, and allies are within reach.

Should the Key fall far away or be with difficult cards, it promises the reverse. The querent's dreams are set to fail, his hopes are denied, and obstacle after obstacle will dog him.

Progressed Meanings:

The Key is a very positive card in and of itself. What follows the Key is almost certainly set to happen. As a rule, it says 'yes' to whatever is to its left, so negative cards become more certain. At best you might find a solution, but you will need to face whatever is augured by the Key.

Obviously the Key can also be real keys. With the Cavalier, the House or the Moon it can be your car, house or office keys respectively. With the Book it can be a password or passcode.

Health: The Key stands for tests and diagnoses, such as MRIs, bone density scans, or specialist screening questionnaires to diagnose communication disorders like autism. It can also show keyhole surgery when it's with the Scythe.

34 – The Fish

King of Diamonds

Keywords:
Income, financial ventures, business

The Fish symbolises the essence affluence.

Two or more fish swimming in the clear blue ocean is the most common representation of this card's emblem. Sometimes we might see a ship in the distance.

When the Fish card falls far away from the significator it means that the querent should expect a lean spell financially. Business ventures will be tested, whilst opportunities to alleviate austerity will prove few or difficult to instigate and pull off.

When the Fish is close by, the querent can expect an upturn in her financial circumstances. She may receive a pay rise. Opportunities frequently appear which, if taken, will bring greater prosperity.

Progressed Meanings:

'Income' is the word most used to describe this card. It shows whatever money you have that comes in regularly, from your salary to your pension to any benefits. When the Fish falls close by to the querent's card there is an opportunity to increase your income, though it normally involves taking on something extra.

If the Stars are by the Fish it can show a windfall. If the Fish is touched by the Sun or the Clover you might just get lucky!

Another meaning of the Fish is depth. It can show deep and rich feelings when it falls with the Heart. But be careful here, as it may simply indicate a great love of the high-life and designer clothing.

The Fish card symbolises liquid. This can be the ocean, a swimming pool (with the Garden), a bath (with the House) and drinks.

Health: The Fish stands for the urinary system, and in fertility questions it represents potency. Otherwise the Fish can show liquids which, with the Clouds, might reveal alcohol abuse.

35 – The Anchor

9 of Spades

Keywords:
Hope, foundation, stable

The Anchor is the essence of hope.

Normally, we see this emblem portrayed as a ship's anchor, which can be seen lying on the shore. Occasionally, more elaborate decks might show it dropped to the seabed.

When the Anchor is with good cards, it promises that your relationships and professional life are being built on strong foundations. Your hopes in these areas are set to be fulfilled. This is a good omen for new romance; it shows you've bagged a keeper.

When the Anchor is with negative cards it shows that you're building on shifting sands. Your job or business might be slated for a setback, and your relationships are with people who will prove fickle. You're left with just your hopes and no certainties.

Progressed Meanings:

The Anchor stands for stability. This is the card that shows something lasting: your relationships, your business, your job security. Concerning the latter, the Anchor can show your long-term aspirations but you'll still need the Moon to get that promotion, or to see if you'll be the new high-flyer, or just to get your foot in the door.

When the Anchor appears in love readings it's a good indicator of whether this is a lasting relationship. Normally the querent will be hoping it is, so delineate the cards carefully, as with negative cards the Anchor shows that the relationship is not long term. This isn't always a bad thing!

The closer the Anchor falls to the querent's card, the stronger it is; you don't want to see the Anchor close by with negative cards.

Health: The Anchor denotes how stable a recovery is. Good cards around the Anchor are a strong sign of a good recovery. Anatomically, it stands for the hips and pelvic bones.

36 – The Cross

6 of Clubs

Keywords:
Hardships, fate, faith

The Cross's essence is suffering.

Normally, the emblem of the Cross is either a cross or (in Catholic countries) a crucifix, normally in gold, and well carved. The Mystical Lenormand shows a Celtic-cross headstone.

This is one of the most negative cards in the deck. It stands for testing times of grief and pain wherever it falls, which can only be mitigated if it falls close to the querent's card. Then it means misery of short duration.

It's a fateful card. Whatever the Cross is touching becomes burdensome and difficult and there isn't much you can do to avoid it.

Progressed Meanings:

In select situations the trials of the Cross can mean an actual test. It's often a test you don't want to take: a performance review, a benefits assessment, or having to retake your driver's licence exam when you turn a certain age. It's something bothersome that can lead to great difficulties if you don't pass.

The Cross stands for religion of any denomination. When the Cross falls after a person card it's not uncommon to find that the person is religious, even a Wiccan high priestess or Jewish rabbi. When it's before a person card it can be someone you've not seen for several years, or simply someone you hate dealing with.

If the Garden comes after the Cross it is often a cemetery or a place someone goes to remember. If the Garden comes first, consider a religious building, food bank or crisis centre.

Do note the cards on either side of the Cross. Whatever is to the Cross's left is diminished and becomes less important; the cards to the right become more important and gain strength.

Health: The Cross indicates being spent. Your energy is drained and you are frequently in pain. It's a debilitating card. In terms of anatomy it stands for the lower back and lumbar discs.

Exercise #1 – Reference Sheet

By now you should have a feel for the cards' meanings. To aid your learning in the coming exercises on building combinations, you should distil those meanings into a few keywords that encapsulate the cards' definitions in your own words. I recommend you aim for two nouns and two adjectives per card. Nouns denote topics, whereas adjectives describe the topic. So for the Birds you may choose grief and journey as nouns and sorrowful and anxious as the adjectives. When a card comes first in a combination, it is similar to a noun, setting a topic within the reading. The cards immediately following that card elaborate on the topic, like a qualifying adjective. For this reason, make sure you a have a noun for both near and far meanings.

Card Themes

Communications

Both the Cavalier and the Letter bring news, the former very soon and in person rather than through a telephone call, text or document, as is the case of the latter. I often find that if the Cavalier is near the querent's card the news is 'close to home' – from or affecting the querent's family, house-mates or closest friends.

The Birds with the Letter can stand for news by way of a telephone call or Skype. The Rod with the Letter can be formal writs and notices, but also can indicate something that causes a debate, and is more often more reflective of the aftermath of news.

Love

The Heart stands for love in general, whilst the Ring brings commitment in a formal sense, and the Anchor strength and a lasting nature.

The Lord and the Lady are the partner cards for heterosexuals, whilst the Cavalier and the Snake fulfil these roles in gay relationships.

The Lily denotes a happy and sexual relationship.

Family and Home

The Lily is the family card whilst the House will show the people you live with, who don't have to be your family. The Storks close to the significator or the House can show a relocation, home improvement or impending change in your domestic life.

The Child is your children, whilst your parents, or an older female and male relative of importance, are the Bear and the Tower. A sibling and son- or daughter-in-law can be the Fish or the Paths, respectively.

When the Birds follow the Child it can predict pregnancy.

Happiness

The Clover (joy), Bouquet (happiness, friendship), Stars (good luck), Heart (love), Lily (peace), Sun (success) and Moon (acclaim) all predict happiness.

The Bear can predict good fortune, but with a warning to avoid jealousy. The Key shows providence.

Work

The Moon stands for your work or job-hunts and how well it is going. The Anchor describes job security. For someone self-employed or heavily involved in retail and trade the Ship is important, too.

The Dog stands for your colleagues and employees. The Fox is your rivals.

Finances

The Fish is your income and business dividends. The Bear shows good fortune.

The Ship (opportunities) and the Anchor (lasting) can give financial indications, too. The House is a good gauge of how comfortable you are.

We look at the Coffin as it can predict a severe financial loss, whilst the Mice shows thefts, which are often monetary.

Warnings

The Snake is a warning you're on complicated ground, and the Fox that you should be very careful, as something is wrong. The Mice indicates loss and theft.

The Scythe shows danger and threats. The Mountain close to the seeker's card it is a sign of an enemy. The Bear with bad cards warns of jealousy, even the evil eye, and is a sign to be careful of whom you confide in.

Sickness

The Tree is the main health card. When close to the significator, or with difficult cards, it can be mitigated by the presence of the House, the Garden, the Paths or the Sun.

The Coffin shows sickness. When the Tower is with the Rod, or by the Clouds or the Coffin, it shows serious and long-term health concerns. The Rod with the Tree or the Coffin can show serious and chronic conditions or relapses.

Trouble

The Clouds always predicts obstacles and tribulations; it brings trouble to other cards, too.

The Snake (need for caution), Coffin (loss, sickness), Scythe (danger, threats), Rod (strife, sickness), Birds (sorrow, stresses), Fox (deceit, wrong), Bear (jealousy), Mountain (enemies, blockages) and Cross (grief) can predict trouble. The Book near the querent's card warns of unforeseen trouble or embarrassment, and the Cavalier and the Letter near negative cards show bad news.

Animals

The Dog stands for pets in general, but specifically your dog, whilst the Fox stands for cats and foxes, too.

The Cavalier is horses, donkeys and ponies, as well as livestock such as cows, pigs, et cetera. The Bear shows bears and wild animals in general.

The Birds stands for domestic and small wild birds up to the size of owls, while the Storks shows birds that are bigger than an owl.

Your pet mice, rats, hamsters, rabbits and guinea pigs, as well as wild rodents, are shown by the Mice. Your pet fish and marine life in general are covered by the Fish card.

The Snake stands for reptiles and exotic pets.

Exercise #2 – Themes

One:

A woman comes to ask questions about her female partner. What cards will you need to look at?

Two:

A male querent is going to a job interview and wonders if he will be successful. What are the key cards?

Three:

Your son's girlfriend has left him and you want to know if they will get back together. What are the key cards?

Exercise #2 – Themes (Answers)

One:

A woman comes to ask questions about her female partner. What cards will you need to look at?

Lady (querent), Snake (partner), Heart, Ring, Anchor and Lily.

Two:

A male querent is going to a job interview and wonders if he will be successful. What are the key cards?

Lord, Moon, Anchor, Sun (success) and Key (aspirations).

Three:

Your son's girlfriend has left him and you want to know if they will get back together. What are the key cards?

Your son is the Child, his girlfriend would be the Paths, and you would examine the Ring, the Anchor and the Heart.

Positive to Neutral to Negative

Imagine a standard ruler, which runs from 0 (positive) to 30 (negative) centimetres. If you took one end to be positive and the other negative, you could plot the 36 cards of the Petit Lenormand along it.

Most of the Petit Lenormand cards would fall somewhere between 10 and 20 centimetres, meaning they are positive-neutral to neutral-negative. Learning this spectrum of influence is crucial for accuracy, and the key to doing simple yes-or-no questions.

Here is a list of the cards, grouped by positivity or negativity:

Positive:

Clover*, Bouquet, Stars*, Heart, Sun, Moon, Key, Fish

Positive-Neutral:

Cavalier, Ship, House, Child, Dog, Storks, Lily, Anchor

Neutral:

Bear, Tower, Garden, Paths, Ring, Letter

Neutral-Negative:

Tree, Snake, Birds, Book

Negative:

Clouds, Coffin, Scythe, Rod, Fox, Mountain, Mice, Cross

Because they are the cards spoken about, the Lord and the Lady have no value on this scale.

The neutral, neutral-positive and neutral-negative cards can be intensified or mitigated by falling with positive or negative cards. For instance, the Letter would become positive with the Fish and the Sun (news of a financial success), but negative with the Coffin and the Mice (news of a financial loss).

* The Clover and the Stars become negative with the Clouds.

People Cards

As well as the Lord and the Lady, there are several cards that can stand for people in your life.

You will have noticed in the cards' meanings that when discussing a card which corresponds to a playing card King or Queen, I said it can describe a man or woman. This is true, but I emphasise that this is in appropriate contexts only. Most of the time the Snake will simply show complications and wrangling, but it can also show a woman, frequently your ex-wife or your ex-husband's new partner, or if you are reading for a lesbian, her partner. The Snake is only a woman when context dictates.

I personally never use the Jacks as people cards apart from the Jack of Spades (Child), who naturally fulfils the role of the querent's children.

Once you know roughly who the person is you build a description – character and appearance – from the cards the person card is touching.

Here's a quick list:

HEARTS:

King (House)

A man who is about the same age or older than the querent such as an older sibling, godfather or mentor.

Queen (Storks)

Often a woman the same age or a bit older than the querent fulfilling a role such as an older sister, godmother or confidante.

SPADES:

King (Lily)

This King is a patron – someone who will help and aid the querent. Otherwise, he is either a young man, such as a lover, or the querent's adult sons (when they have several grandchildren).

Queen (Bouquet)

This Queen is a woman who provides nurturing support to the querent. She can be an aunt, a mother-in-law and sometimes a stepmother; otherwise she is a young woman, lover or the querent's adult daughters.

DIAMONDS:

King (Fish):

This King can be a man who is younger than the querent, such as a brother, a male cousin, a son-in-law or even a business partner.

Queen (Paths)

This woman is sometimes a sibling or a cousin, especially a much younger one, or a daughter-in-law – someone who has no formal role in the querent's life.

CLUBS:

King (Clouds)

This King stands for a man in your life who traditionally has a difficult role. It can be your ex-partner, your ex-partner's new man, your step-father or simply someone causing trouble for you.

Queen (Snake)

This Queen stands for the other woman. She can be your ex-partner, your partner's new wife, a stepmother or a woman you don't much like.

PART TWO: Combining and Reading the Cards Together

Building Combinations

As you progress through this book, you will notice that I frequently allude to the Petit Lenormand as being like a language. In fact, the way we read this deck is quite linguistic, and the cards act like a shorthand we are transcribing when we give a reading.

As in late 19th century stenographic systems, we are reading what a symbol (for example, a thick or thin line) means, rather than what it is doing or what it reminds us of. Because of this, in the Petit Lenormand we read what the Fox and the Bear mean and combine the meanings. We are not particularly interested in what either look to be doing, or whether they face each other in the reading.

This is called combination reading. I do not believe it is useful to give the student a list of combinations, as actual meanings can vary from reading to reading, and context is paramount. I have included some useful combinations to commit to memory in the appendix. In this chapter, we will look at how to derive combinations.

Card combinations can be formed in the following ways:

1. By being near to or far from the significator and other key cards.

2. By cards that are touching.

3. By direction of the emblems.

3. By correlation to other cards, usually derived through methods such as counting or knighting.

4. By chaining, for example, love issues can be derived by reading the cards between the Heart, the Ring and the Anchor, then considering the testimonies together.

We will look at these points throughout this chapter. Numbers 1 and 4 will be covered in further detail in the next chapter on the Grand Tableau.

Proximity – Being near to or far from the significator and other key cards

The oldest instructions for the Petit Lenormand, circa 1850, outline the cards' meanings by proximity using the terms 'near' and 'far'. You will notice in the previous chapter that I delineated the meanings in this manner. Whilst we will cover near and far in depth in the next chapter, you should understand that proximity is used in smaller readings as well – in fact, it can be crucial: proximity gives you a card's meaning.

In terms of smaller deals it's useful to consider proximity in the following ways:

Cards are near to cards they touch. Two or more cards away is far.

Thus in this line of five cards:

A – B – C – D – E

Card B is near Cards A and C, but is far from Cards D and E, with the latter being the farther.

As the middle card, C has no card more than two places from it. It is, therefore, often given special status, such as a theme or hinge.

The dealing of the significator or key cards (Clouds, Tree, Coffin, Scythe, Ring) introduces the importance of proximity and can alter meanings. For example, Clouds + Stars means the Stars signifies bad luck.

In this line of cards:

Lady – Dog – Birds – Clouds – Key

If we were reading for a woman she would be symbolised by the Lady, who is close to the Dog.

The Clouds is not near the Lady, but is close to the Birds and the Key, and thus affects their meanings. As the Key is far from the Lady and near to the Clouds, it would symbolise complete failure and misfortune. Similarly, the short sorrow of the Birds is made more lasting by being beside the Clouds.

If neither the significator nor key cards which have influencing qualities such as the Clouds or the Tree appear, use a middle-level meaning in your readings. This is often a blend of the cards' near and far meanings.

For instance, in this reading:

Letter – Dog – Birds – Bouquet – Sun

No modification card has appeared and only the Birds has a particularly problematic meaning. I would read it as anxieties or worries, as opposed to short-lived sorrow.

This is where meaning 'weight' comes in. If you are asking for information about that day or that week, the cards' meanings are not going to be as heavy as in a reading covering eight weeks' time or more.

Thus the Birds is more likely to show a telephone call, or being in a flap or busy, than short-lived sorrow or a surprising trip in the week ahead. In readings covering a longer period, the Birds is more often anxieties, rather than just telephone calls.

Attendance – By what cards it is touching

Linking card meanings forms combinations into a statement. That statement is discerned in the appropriate context, e.g. love, finances, family or work. Each of the thirty-six symbols contains specific concepts or meanings which act like lighthouses leading you towards and threading together meaning.

The most basic form of combination outside of proximity is when cards fall side-by-side. This is called attendance. For example, Card B is attended by Cards A and C. Common numbers for attendance combinations are two to three and sometimes up to five cards. Attendance can also create combinations vertically and diagonally.

At a later stage we will be building combinations in other ways, through mirroring, counting and knighting but the purpose of this section is to cement two ideas:

1. Attendance elaborates on proximity.

If the Sun is near away from the significator it stands for success and overcoming challenges. If it is attended by the Cross, there is difficulties and challenges that will bring pain and hardship also.

2. Attendance is based on ordering.

For consistency, we will remain with our hypothetical scenario of the Sun being near the significator. If it is attended by the Cross, card order will denote how any difficulty manifests.

If you have:

Cross – Sun

This means that after some short lived difficulties that have taxed the seeker a period of success and renewal begins. But if you have:

Sun – Cross

This combination shows a period of success ends and challenges the querent is not able to overcome result in hardship, bringing pain and grief in the short term.

As you will remember, the Cross diminishes whatever is to its left, but magnifies the importance of what is to its right.

Thus we reach a very, very important rule:

A + B is not the same as B + A.

Whilst both combinations will be similar, because A will always mean X, and B will always mean Y, which card comes first will have important implications.

A simple analogy is:

Card 1 is like a noun. Nouns denote a person, object or place.

Card 2 is like an adjective. Adjectives describe or seek to qualify a noun.

Thus with Cards A – B, we learn about Card A from Card B. If we reverse them so the order is B – A, we learn about Card B from Card A.

Let's look at a few examples:

Letter – Coffin

The Letter always signifies news and messages, often in written form. The Coffin indicates a loss or a sickness. So what would the Coffin tell us about the Letter?

Think about it before reading on.

It is bad news. This could be news (Letter) of termination (Coffin) or a rejection letter. It could also be a sick note, or a medical report – usually with negative implications. Because of the nature of the Coffin this could be a sign that the letter or document is lost.

Let's reverse the order now.

Coffin – Letter

As before, we are dealing with loss or a sickness and news – but what does the Letter say about the Coffin?

Spend a few minutes thinking before reading my suggestions.

This could be a death notice such as an obituary in the newspaper, or simply being told someone has become sick. It can be a sign of diagnosis, such as being told what is wrong and its long-term ramifications.

Adding in more cards

Quite naturally, this rule can be expanded to factor in more cards. There is nothing wrong with two cards per se, but the nature of this deck is such that three cards are often the best minimum to get a decent statement. Three cards are good for daily draws and yes-or-no readings. So how would three cards work?

A – B – C.

A sets the subject.

B tells us about A.

C tells us more about whatever A – B denotes.

Let's return to the previous example involving the Letter and the Coffin. We will add in the Cross, as we have already explored that card's implications.

Letter – Coffin – Cross

Here the Cross is telling us about the Letter – Coffin. The Cross diminishes the Letter – Coffin's statement. This would be bad news that causes pain but with little you can do about it, such as a notice of termination or a medical report making recommendations you do not agree with.

If we switch the Coffin and the Letter around:

Coffin – Letter – Cross

This could be a difficult or final diagnosis, and the Cross would be cutting off treatment options, so it is not uncommon to show that you'll be learning that someone is chronically ill. As the Coffin can show loss and the Letter news, followed by the Cross this can be a lost appeal, too.

If we wanted to add in another card:

A – B – C – D

D here tells us more about whatever A – B – C denotes.

Letter – Coffin – Cross – Storks

Now the Storks is telling us about Letter – Coffin – Cross. Remember that the card falling after the Cross becomes extra important. You could be forced to leave a job or significantly change your life (Cross – Storks) after notice of termination or the filing of a medical report (Letter – Coffin – Cross).

Coffin – Letter – Cross – Storks

Here the Storks is telling us about Coffin – Letter – Cross. This would be forcing you to change something because of a difficult diagnosis or to move on, unhappily, after news of a loss (Coffin – Letter – Cross).

Each subsequent card elaborates on the cards that have gone before. Because of the importance of card order we do not allow the cards' designs to influence us.

Vertical Attendance

In some combinations, you will have cards forming combinations vertically – from top to bottom.

A simple rule to remember: Cards above influence cards below them.

So if you see:

Fox
Letter

The Fox is influencing the Letter. The Fox stands for deceit and shows a need for caution. The Letter is news and communications.

We have an attempt to deceive (Fox) through communications (Letter). Basically, don't believe everything you read or hear.

If we reverse it:

Letter
Fox

The Letter is influencing the Fox. This would show news (Letter) that is confusing or has a mistake in it (Fox) rather than being outright misleading.

Exercise #3 – Attendance Practise

Part One:

Combine the following cards to get an answer.

If you struggle, answer them as follows:

Cards:
Your Keywords: [noun] + [adjective]
Your answer: [a single statement]

a. Ship – Dog
b. Child – Coffin
c. Lord – Scythe
d. Fox – Snake
e. Snake – Fox
f. Tower – Lily
g. Cross – Moon
h. Clover – Birds
i. Tree – Garden
j. Clouds – Paths
k. Book – Cavalier

Part Two:

Combine the following:

a. Fish – Letter – Mice

b. Dog
   Garden

c. Lady – Dog – Ship – Birds – Lord

Exercise #3 – Attendance Practise (Answers)

Part One:

a. Ship – Dog
Travel with or to a friend.

b. Child – Coffin
Childhood illnesses or loss of support.

c. Lord – Scythe
Aggressive man; a man suddenly appears.

d. Fox – Snake
A deceitful woman.

e. Snake – Fox
A clever woman.

f. Tower – Lily
Older male; separation from the family.

g. Cross – Moon
Growing reputation; end of a job search.

h. Clover – Birds
Double the luck.

i. Tree – Garden
Convalescent home; forest or woods.

j. Clouds – Paths
Bad choice, despair.

k. Book – Cavalier
Unexpected visitor or news.

Part Two:

a. Fish – Letter – Mice
Stolen or lost cheque; missing money on a bank statement.

b. Dog
   Garden
Leader of the pack; fraternity.

c. Lady – Dog – Ship – Birds – Lord
A woman and her friend/dog are travelling to see a man.

By Direction

When you grow in confidence, you can, and should, begin to look at direction. When we talk of direction, we are talking about making inferences based on the direction of the emblems shown on the cards. It is important to note, however, that direction cannot overrule either proximity or order.

For example, imagine we deal:

Fox – Snake

We know that the Fox symbolises deceit. Whatever follows the Fox is wrong. Thus, the Snake symbolises what is wrong. This will never change regardless of which way either cards face. As the Snake can stand for a woman, we could read this as a deceitful and scheming woman.

Why would this woman want to deceive you? To discern this little detail, we could look at what the Snake is facing. Both the *Dondorf* (the deck used in this book) and the *Blaue Eule* patterns portray the Snake facing left. Thus, as she looks at the Fox, we say she wants to defraud you (the Fox's meaning).

No. 194115 Mlle Lenormand, published by Piatnik, shows the Snake facing right. Thus, if you were using that deck, you would look at whatever follows the Snake. If this were the House or the Book, you could say she wanted something within your home or private information, respectively.

Imagine when you deal the following cards:

Dog – Scythe – Rod – Heart

The direction is very useful here. Why? The answer is in the Scythe and the Rod. It's a combination where it often doesn't matter which one comes first – its arguments and strife can play out violently, which can be or lead to physical violence.

We know that the Rod represents a threat because it follows the Scythe. But, why is this? Does the tip of the blade point to the Dog or the Rod? If it were the former, both the violence and danger would come directly from whomever the Dog stood for. You might antagonise him (Rod + Heart), and he will hit you. If, however, it pointed to the Rod (as above), the danger would come from whatever was said (Rod). In that case, the Dog might run his mouth off and get you into a fight.

As you can see, we did not change the order of our interpretation. It all stemmed from the Dog. Direction should not change the order of the cards. It only provides the extra details.

By Correlation

Correlation is best used selectively and only when needed. The Petit Lenormand, like most traditional cartomancy practices with playing cards, is very lean and can easily be overworked.

Some methods of correlation are:

Counting

This is one of the oldest methods, several versions of which survive. You can count in fives, sevens, nines and thirteens. I tend to use the ninth and every thirteenth card method, which was popularised on the continent in the 19th and early 20th centuries.

Here you can take your key card as 1 and count along to the 9th card. Combine cards 1 and 9. Then take the card immediately to the right of card 9 as card 10 and count to 13. Combine card 13 with whatever card 1 + 9 meant. Take the card to the right of card 13 as 10 and find the next 13, which explains 1 + 9 + 13.

Eventually, you will land back on card 1, thus ending the count. I do not do this in every reading, and when I do, I limit it to the significator.

Mirroring (also called Reflecting)

Mirroring, or reflecting, adds extra detail. It is done by 'folding' a row either vertically or horizontally. So in a row of eight cards, cards 1 and 8 mirror each other, cards 2 and 7 mirror each other, and so on.

If we look at these cards:

Lord – Letter – Ship – Bouquet – Fish

A man (Lord) has received some news (Letter) that has given him financial (Fish) and business opportunities (Ship), which he is very happy about (Bouquet).

The Fish is far from the Lord, so its business and monetary meanings would be lessened, but as the Bouquet touches the Fish it still brings some wealth. The Ship, being two cards from the Lord, could also indicate travel.

Here the Lord mirrors the Fish, indicating a man who is wealthy or in business. The Letter mirrors the Bouquet, showing news that makes you happy, or an invitation. Thus we have more specifics we could add to our earlier summary.

We could say that a businessman (Lord + Fish) has received an invitation (Letter + Bouquet) from abroad to travel (Ship), which will bring him new opportunities (Ship) that are very promising (Bouquet) financially (Fish).

Knighting

Knighting is based on the movement of a knight in the game of chess. Thus:

Two positions left or right and then one up or down;
Two positions up or down and then one left or right;

One position left or right and then two up or down.

It can be used in spreads where there are three or more rows, and thus is mostly used with the Grand Tableau.

In my experience, knighting can be of use when you are looking at specific life areas such as work, where you would knight from the Moon and the Anchor (the two traditional business cards) to gain clarification or extra detail on the predictions given by the attending cards. Of note would be the Moon knighted to the Anchor, or any card that could be knighted by both the Moon and the Anchor.

Again, I recommend that you use these techniques selectively. Otherwise, you will just contradict yourself.

By Theme

When cards fall between two cards of the same theme, e.g. the Moon and the Anchor for work, or the House and the Lily for family and home life, this is called a chain.

Read the cards between the theme cards as if they are in horizontal attendance, and keep your reading to the context of the theme cards.

If a female client pulls the following cards in her reading:

Moon – Birds – Lady – Rod – Anchor

The Birds, the Lady and the Rod are read as relating to employment issues within this chain. It indicates that professionally (Moon and Anchor) the querent is set to face some disappointments or sorrow caused by unpleasantness in her job (Birds – Lady – Rod).

If we use the same middle cards with another theme:

Ring – Birds – Lady – Rod – Heart

Now we're talking about love. This shows that the querent's relationship will end (Ring to the left) because of conflict (Birds – Lady – Rod), resulting in upset and heartache (Rod – Heart). As the Ring is only two cards away, reconciliation is not out of the question. For a deeper view we would have to look at the Anchor to see whether this is hopeful.

PART THREE: Laying the Cards

Spreads

In this final part of the book, we will look at how to perform actual readings.

Our first spread is the traditional Grand Tableau, which uses all thirty-six cards. This is a layout best done to review your life over a set period of time, such as three months to a year. After this we look at the Modern Tableau. This is good for answering complex questions, where you need to review the past, present and future.

We will then look at Fan spreads, which can be used to answer specific queries, from simple yes-or-no questions to in-depth multi-part situations.

Then we will look at the 3 x 3, which can be used to get a general picture of a short period of time, such as two to eight weeks into the future.

Finally, we conclude with the pyramid spread, which can be used to pinpoint origins and root causes of problems and situations.

Please note: all names in the following examples have been changed in order to protect privacy.

The Traditional Grand Tableau

The Grand Tableau, meaning 'big picture', is the traditional way of reading the Petit Lenormand. You may choose never to use it, but if you want to learn the Lenormand method you will need to learn how to do one. Why? It is how the method was developed and what it was designed for.

In the coming pages, we will be using the 8 x 4 + 4 (four rows of eight and one row of four) layout, as that is my preferred variation. You can use all the techniques I outline in the 9 x 4 (four rows of nine) and 6 x 6 (six rows of six) variations.

Why are there several versions? In the 18th and 19th centuries many fortune-tellers in Europe used a pack of thirty-two playing cards (piquet) and laid them out in four rows of eight. The 9 x 4 layout recreates that symmetry. The 8 x 4 + 4 acknowledges the addition of the four sixes. The 8 x 4 + 4 is what is used in the Philippe Lenormand instruction sheet, circa 1850.

I want to remind you that what follows is my preferred way. Later you can experiment and try other methods. It is important to remember that tableaus predate the Petit Lenormand, and come from playing card reading in general, so there are various ways of breaking them up – some are very similar to the ways we are discussing, others different.

Many readers break their tableaus into past, present and future. This is a modern innovation and we look at this after the traditional version. I reserve this concept for in-depth or multi-part questions.

How I Read the Traditional Tableau

Over time, I have developed a way of reading the tableau that incorporates what I learned from my teachers and what I learned through practice, trial and error. The latter is important. For example, some practices my Aunt showed me never worked for me or my clientele. Similarly, practices that work for me may not have not done for all of my students. You are free to adapt my methods or to ignore them totally.

Some of the techniques are adaptations of techniques I discovered from playing card readers. For example, one of my teachers used counting extensively with playing card tableaus. As Petit Lenormand is a method of reading playing cards, this method adapts easily. I have found counting from the significator both important and useful.

As such, over time you can adapt or dispense methods you first learn. My recommendation is to keep it simple; keep the focus on the cards, not on the techniques. Whilst the following methods might seem complicated when written down, in practice you will find they are fluid and quick.

Here is step-by-step breakdown of my standard approach:

1. I cut the shuffled deck in two and read the bottom cards of each pile. The cut very often shows me an important dynamic, e.g. Ship – Lily could be longing (Ship) for happiness (Lily). I note the suits, and if two different suits appear, I consider their combination. Here is a strong hint of the energy unfolding.

2.   Next, I read the first three cards laid out. These are a message to the querent. If the third card is either the Clouds, the Fox, the Mice or the Cross, you should include the fourth card. This is because these four cards have meanings associated with cards falling both to the left and to the right of them.

3.   Third, I read the four corners. Corners act like boundaries, showing overriding influences or topics in the appearing period. Seeing a person card in a corner position means the person is affecting the querent's future directly. If the card representing the querent falls in a corner, his or her actions will carry extra weight in the coming months. Big changes are forecasted.

4.   I look at how the cards have fallen around the querent's card. From this, I discern which cards are near and which are far. I do the same for the Clouds, too.

5.   Focusing on the significator, I note how many cards are to its left, its right, above and below. The cards to the significator's left are weakened (for good or bad), and the cards to the significator's right are intensified (again, for good or bad). Cards that fall above the querent's card are amplified, and cards that fall below are weakened. Again, this determines good or bad.

Next, I check the middle of the tableau. In the 8 x 4 + 4, that is cards 12, 13, 20 and 21. These cards make the most combinations. What theme do they share? For example, if the House, the Lily, the Dog and the Sun fall here, domestic happiness is emphasised. Similarly, the Coffin, the Tree, the Birds and the Mountain would point to difficulties and health issues. Check the suits, too.

6. I read the cards that fall in the last row of four cards. They describe an important, or triggering, event that can sometimes explain or give context to the other parts of the tableau.

7. Now I begin to look more closely at the card that stands for the person for whom I am reading. As always, this is the Lord for a man and the Lady for a woman. I note which cards touch it, especially the diagonals, as these function just as the tableau's four corners in step 3.

8. I will count from the querent's card, using a count of nine and every thirteenth.

9. I then turn my attention to any cards that the significator faces horizontally. This row of cards describes topics that usually happen within four weeks' time.

10. Finally, I do what I refer to as 'the general reading'. This is when I cover topics such as relationships, family, work, money and well-being. We do this by recalling the themes, e.g. for relationships, you look at the Heart, the Ring and the Anchor cards. I also look at the Clouds as this card shows where the biggest problems come from.

For each card in a theme we:

    A. Note their proximity; that is your first testimony.
    B. Look at their boundaries (diagonal cards).
    C. Read the cluster (card immediately to its left, right, above and below)
    D. Note any chains between theme cards.

If needed we can also:

  E. Mirror the cards, as necessary, for an explanation of any past incidents or important context.
  F. Knight, if needed, for a further look into the future.

  By step 10, we have normally reviewed most if not all the cards. You can then ask the client if they have any questions and look at the appropriate cards to answer them.

Additional Techniques

Before we begin I will touch on two techniques I use in the example reading: mirroring and counting.

Mirroring

Mirroring is when you take a card and combine it with another card that reflects its position in the formation.

As long as the card is not one of the last four cards, it will reflect three others. We do this by 'folding' the tableau horizontally, vertically and diagonally. For brevity, I will use the cards' numerical value (i.e. 1 for Cavalier, 10 for Scythe, et cetera) in the following illustration

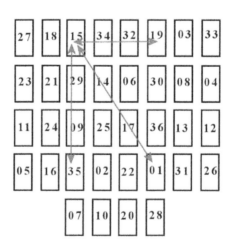

152

In our example above, card 15, the Bear, is in the third place in the top row. Horizontally it reflects 35, the Anchor, the third card in the bottom row of eight. The Bear also reflects 19, the Tower, at the far right of the top row. Diagonally it reflects 1, the Cavalier.

Looking at what the significator reflects in a Grand Tableau is something I have found useful for discerning the atmosphere around the querent; it hints at the past, too.

Counting

Counting was common in reading tableaus of any deck before the mid-20th century. Most readers would have counted from several key cards, such as the wish card and house card. Personally, I only like to count from the significator in my tableaus with the Petit Lenormand.

I use a count of nine, and every thirteenth card. Other readers count in threes, fives and sevens.

Here's how you do it:

a. Take the Lady (29) card as the significator and card 1, going right. Count until you reach card 9.

In the tableau below the Bouquet (9) is the ninth card. This shows us that the querent's happiness in daily life is an issue.

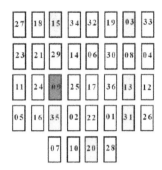

b. Take the card immediately to the right of card 9 as card 10, and find card 13.

c. Take the card immediately to the right of card 13 as a new 10 and count along to find the next thirteenth card. Repeat this until you land back on the querent's card.

Our thirteenth cards are: 13 – Child, 35 – Anchor, 31 – Sun, 20 – Garden, 15 – Bear, and 3 – Ship.

We read these cards as a narrative concerning the topic set by card 9, the Bouquet, noting their positions in the tableau and how the cards around them affect them. It is important to remember the cards' meanings are still determined by their proximity to the significator and the Clouds. For example, as the Sun has fallen at some distance from the Lady it will not show success, but disappointment and struggles.

The counted cards indicate that the client's associates (Child) will have to help her (Anchor) overcome difficulties (Sun) because of disloyal (Garden) and jealous people (Bear) who will threaten her endeavours (Ship).

Division:

I have found that the Grand Tableau primarily covers events concerning the seeker's immediate circumstances and for up to twelve weeks. In tableaus covering six months or longer you will find, frequently, that many of the events augured will take place within three months. This, I believe, is a direct side effect of the pace of modern life.

Ten years ago the news the Cavalier brought would often appear within a week or two, these days it's often a day or two.

When you have an important few weeks coming up, you may wish to do a tableau centred solely on that month. The following technique, which I call division, is useful for a tableau covering eight weeks or fewer, and replaces step ten (the 'the general reading'). In a tableau covering just a month one will seldom wish to cover all the key life areas.*

Division is a way of breaking the tableau up into four sections, according to the flow of time. So whatever timeframe you are using it must be divided into four.

As this technique was originally done with a 32-card pack, the division is comprised solely of four rows of eight.

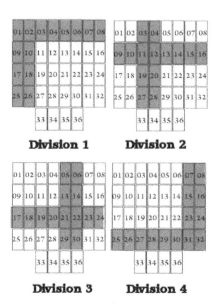

Division 1:

The first row and the first two columns.

Division 2:

The second row and the third and fourth columns.

Division 3:

The third row and the fifth and sixth columns.

Division 4:

The fourth row and the seventh and eighth columns.

For example, this year I wanted to look at February 2015. As 2015 is not a leap year there are just 28 days in the month, so I can say each division covers seven days. The breakdown would look as follows:

Division 1:

Showed events taking place between February 1-7.

Division 2:

Showed events taking place between February 8-14.

Division 3:

Showed events taking place between February 15-21.

Division 4:

Showed events taking place between February 22-28.

Now that you know what timeframe each division represents, you simply read in order. So you start with the first row, and then you read the first two columns (top to bottom). Once that is done you move to the second division and so on.

Division allows us to break the tableau into manageable chunks from an interpretive level. I have genuinely found that events augured do occur in within the timeframe associated with the appropriate division about 90 per cent of the time. However, life is not neat and division does not set an absolute itinerary that Father Time will follow.

For example, I had Fox – Letter as the last two cards of division two. I did not find out that there was something wrong with my telephone until February 16. Even though the problem did start a few days prior, one must be flexible.

*Should you do a tableau covering just one month, I recommend only using steps 1, 3, 4, 6 as outlined earlier in this chapter and then division technique.

Example Reading

George is a junior social worker in his late twenties. He is a close friend of one of my brothers-in-law who booked a reading for him with me as a birthday present. At the time of the reading, he was single but hoped that that would change in the near future. His tableau covered six months.

Step One

After I had shuffled my cards, I cut them into two stacks. The cut was:

Snake – Stars

We can see from this that wrangling over direction will be an important dynamic. Clubs followed by Hearts always keeps us on our toes. Difficulties intrude directly.

Step Two

I now laid out the full Grand Tableau. Here are George's cards as they fell:

We ignore the remainder of the tableau and read the first three cards drawn. This is a message to George. Often these first cards act like a daily draw, referring to something that has already happened or will happen on the day of the reading, or very shortly after (within a few days).

George's first three cards were:

Storks – Lord – Moon

These show that George has a change in his professional status for all to see. George told me he had been offered a new job the day before, but he had not yet accepted it and did not want to say why. Based on these cards, I doubted he would decline.

Step Three

Now, it was time to turn my attention to the four corner cards. I read card 1 in combination with card 32, and card 8 with card 25. You can also read them clockwise, starting from the top left. These cards show events or topics which are often overriding factors in whatever else the reading covers. They do not set a context that you have to relate everything else to; there will be other things going on in the cards and in the querent's life. Still, the corners tend to be influential or important over the coming months.

Sometimes, the two pairs will share a theme. If they do, that's great; when they do not, that's fine also.

George's four corner cards are:

Storks – Fox; Tower – Clover

These show that George will be cautious and discriminating in the changes he makes to his life (Storks – Fox). Had the Fox come first, it would be making the wrong changes. There is a joyful turn of events in his life coming, too (Tower – Clover).

Step Four

Next we locate the querent's card. For George this is the Lord.

What is near and what is far

Any card touching the significator is very near. In this tableau, those cards are the Moon, the Key, the Ship, the House and the Storks. These cards contain the full weight in terms of 'near' meanings.

The Sun, the Ring, the Fish, the Stars, the Garden and the Anchor are two cards away from the Lord. These are near but will take their meanings in a less intense manner than those just one place away. For example, the Birds will still signify sorrow, but it's not as strong and possibly even more transitory than if the Birds was only one card away.

Falling three places away are the Heart, the Cavalier, the Birds, the Cross, the Clouds, the Coffin and the Bear. These cards are not near. The Birds here will show general stresses or, with good cards, a day out rather than a trip.

The Lady, the Bouquet, the Book, the Child and the Snake are all four places away. The Lily, the Paths, the Mice and the Scythe are five places away. All of these are far away.

Cards four places away will take the cards' far meanings, just not as strongly as those five places away. The Birds would show a surprising and pleasant trip if it were five places away, but if it were four places away, it would be less of a surprise or not quite so pleasant.

At six places away from the Lord, the Tower, the Mountain, the Rod and the Fox are the cards farthest away. These cards contain the full weight in terms of their 'far' meanings.

Near and far from the Clouds

The Clouds has fallen in the last row of four cards. Obviously, this means that there are just two cards to its left and one to its right. There is nothing below it.

We can take the Coffin, the Letter, the Cross, the Child and the Snake as clouded; the Bear, too, but to a lesser extent, as it is two positions away.

The Tree, the Stars, the Fish, the Birds, the Book, the Mice and the Scythe are near (two positions away) the Clouds but above it. We have to exercise caution with these seven cards, as they are clouded (within one to two spaces of the Clouds), but they are influencing rather than influenced by the Clouds.

In my experience, cards in such a position tend to manifest problems less directly. For example, George might experience problems being paid. He might be underpaid or receive his salary late or incur unexpected charges.

Step Five

The cards to the significator's left are weakened (for good or bad) and the cards to the significator's right are intensified (again, for good or bad). George has just four cards to his significator's left. Cards that fall above the querent's card are amplified and cards below are weakened. Again, this is for good or bad. No cards are above the Lord, here.

A card in the upper right is more influential than a card in the lower right. If the Clouds were in the lower left it would thus be less problematic than if it were in the lower right. This nuance is crucial with the Clouds, the Ring, the House and the Lily, which gain importance depending on whether they are left or right, above or below the querent's card.

In our example, the Ring and the Clouds are both to the Lord's right, and the Lily is in the same horizontal row as the querent's card. The House is to his lower left. As the Clouds is to the Lord's right, it is more troublesome, but far away. The Ring being to his right is a strong testimony of a future relationship, whilst the Lily and the House here are neutral.

George has much going on during the next six months (more cards to his right). All the negative cards are to his right, showing a mixture of good and bad events, but these are all within his control (having no cards above the Lord).

Step Six

Not every reader who uses the 8 x 4 + 4 gives special importance to the last four cards. You can just treat them as a row of four with no more influence or importance than the four rows of eight cards.

As they sit 'below' the tableau, they are, symbolically, like the deepest soil. Modern physics has hypothesised something fortune-tellers have always known: Time is multi-dimensional. We build layers; as such, the bottom layer can be both the most distant past and the immediate present (in another dimension). The last row is just like this. The cards describe an important, or triggering, event that can sometimes explain or give context to other parts of the tableau, much like a quintessence, if you will.

For this reason, when you first read them, forget everything else. Just take them as four cards. Read them as a sentence.

In our tableau, the last four cards are:

Bear – Coffin – Clouds – Snake

These four cards show that an older, important person in George's life has a complicated and problematic illness. George's mother had been unwell.

We can get further information. We do this by adding in extra cards and interpreting them in the context of the statement.

To learn more about cards 33 and 34, we read cards 27 and 28 (Tree and Letter in this tableau) and then cards 5 and 6 (Heart and Lady). For cards 35 and 36, we read cards 29 and 30 (Cross and Child) and then cards 3 and 4 (Moon and Sun). I do not recommend you do this in every reading.

I did these for George, and we learned that his mother would be referred to (Tree – Letter) and treated by a female doctor, successfully (Moon – Sun). The Moon and the Sun revealed this was a reason George had not yet accepted this role. He was worried about not being around for his mother.

Step Seven

I now look closer at the card which stands for George: 28 – the Lord. We are particularly interested in the cards that immediately touch this card. As the Lord was the second card dealt, there are no cards above him. This means there are only two diagonal cards. All diagonal cards function like the four corners of a tableau: boundaries, overriding influences on the card being reviewed.

George's boundaries are the House and the Key. He is grounded and secure in his domestic affairs. George also likes to keep things 'just so'. He needs to maintain this and thus it will be a great influence (being boundaries). Why? Look at the cluster around the Lord. He is set to relocate (Storks) and move due to career opportunities (Ship, Moon). George's new job is clearly not local, which he confirmed.

As the Ship is just one card away from the Lord, we can be sure George will have a holiday soon, too.

Step Eight

It's time now to count from the Lord. This will show us an important issue or topic in George's life. I use a count of nine, and every thirteenth card. Other readers count in threes, fives and sevens.

In our tableau the Ship is the ninth card. This shows us that travel is a focus.

George's six 'thirteenth' cards are the Bouquet, the Garden, the Book, the Dog, the Child and the Coffin.

We read these cards as a narrative concerning the topic set by card 9, the Ship, noting their positions in the tableau and how the cards around them affect them. For example, as the Dog has fallen near the Clouds, it will take on a clouded meaning.

These cards show that George will travel (Ship) to a very beautiful (Bouquet) location (Garden). George will enjoy his destination and also the company. However, the Book falling before the Dog shows that George has not met one of the companions before. One individual (Dog) will not think well of George (Child). As it's the Dog it could be the hotel staff. This will sour (for George) the trip a bit, and they will not form a good relationship (Child + Coffin). I told George that you cannot be everyone's friend and people clash. The Coffin was nearer to the Dog, rather than the Garden; this issue will only concern this one person rather than the whole holiday. He should not let it trouble him too much.

Step Nine

Now, I was ready to look at the coming few weeks. In my deck, the Lord faces right. So we can read the Moon, the Sun, the Heart, the Lady, the Lily and the Tower cards as events taking place in the next few weeks. It is important to remember that the entire tableau covers the present and the future. We just read this row as being more immediate.

Here we see confirmation of George's professional success (Moon + Sun). It will bring him a rise in status at work and emotional satisfaction. He will also successfully (Sun) win the affection of a woman (Heart + Lady). She will become his lover (Lady + Lily) ending his current bachelorhood and bringing further happiness (Lily + Tower). Whenever the Tower ends the line free of negative cards, I have found it is an auspicious sign of making positive strides in your life. George had much to look forward to.

Step Ten

The 'general reading' is where we cover the areas of interest for the client. For 90% of querents, this is love, home and family, finances, employment, and well-being. I find that proceeding in this order flows well. I also look at the Clouds. The Clouds shows us where we can expect our biggest problems. Should the Letter and the Cavalier not be connected to any key areas, I read these, too, as news.

My interpretation derives first from the card's proximity to the significator and Clouds cards and then by what attends the card.

As you know, cards are attended by whatever they touch. I find that the diagonal cards (boundary cards) are quite important for discerning the influences on the topic. The cluster talks more about events that usually arise out of the boundary cards. Usually, this is more than enough information.

If needed, I will mirror the card. Mirroring gives context and usually hints at past events. In contrast, if I knight, this usually talks about future events or trajectories.

This brings us to an important factor. We are restricted to the cards as they have fallen. Sometimes your clients will press for extra information. Look at what the cards say, and say only what you see.

For clarity and to help your understanding, I will examine the Clouds using the step-by-step approach above.

Clouds:

The Clouds card is to the right of George's card, showing problems of a more serious nature. It is, however, both far from his card and below it; this indicates troubles George can overcome with diligence.

Due to its position, the Clouds card has just two boundary cards: the Letter and the Child. I told George he should expect some problems with his home or mobile phone in the coming months. Unfortunately, as the Letter is to the left of the Clouds, he would also have bad news communicated to him. George does not have children, so the Child is just someone close to him whom he trusts. Unfortunately, this person will not be in a position to help him.

From the cluster, we can see that the bad news will be about a financial setback (Coffin), which causes George hardship and grief (Cross) and will restrict him for a time (Snake).

As the Clouds has fallen in the bottom row of four cards, it does not mirror any other cards. This is somewhat unfortunate; mirroring would give us a back story.

Thus, I knighted from the Clouds. This brought the Tree, the Fish and the Book into play. Connecting the Clouds to both the Tree and the Coffin could indicate health issues. This likely referred to his mother, whom we had already touched on. However, the Fish also spoke about finances. Therefore, I read the Tree as a past (or concurrent) problem. When I explained this to George, he knew what this was about. It was a dispute he was having about hidden costs (Fish and Book).

I advised George that the cards revealed that this would be his biggest problem area. Unfortunately, it looked like he would not win the dispute and would be required to make some sort of payment (Clouds to Fish) that was larger than he expected (Clouds to Book).

With this statement in mind, and the Fish being two cards from the Clouds, I told George that now would be a good time to start considering saving and better managing his money (Clouds being two cards from the Bear) as this trouble could affect his credit history (Child knight to Fish). To be forewarned is to be forearmed.

Now, we will look at love, family, money, work and well-being.

Love:

For relationships, the key cards are the Heart, the Ring and the Anchor, which denote love, commitment and the relationship's endurance, respectively. You will also need to note the partner's card, which here is the Lady and the Lily in conjunction to it. All cards touching these must be read. In addition, chains, and knighting if needed, can be used.

George is single. When your client is single, mirroring the Heart is a good idea. It gives us useful context. For George, the Heart mirrors both the Letter and the Cross. George had some heartache when his feelings were not reciprocated. However, the Sun shows us that he has not let this dampen his spirits too much.

Luckily for George, he has developments in love coming (Bouquet = dates, introductions and Heart = a relationship). This is the shape of a woman (Lady) to whom George will be introduced (Cavalier + Bouquet) and find himself falling in love with (Sun). The Lily to the right of the Lady shows that she will become his lover.

This will help George get over previous sorrow in a relationship (Birds by the Ring). It will prove a strong and deep (Heart, Stars) bond for everyone to see (Moon). The resulting relationship is very secure (Key) and strong (Sun). It will be based on deep feelings (Fish). George will be surprised at how quickly things progress (Cavalier).

On the long-term front, he would even consider living with her (Anchor by the House and Garden). However, the two of them should take their time getting to know each other (Dog is more than two cards away).

George's card fell so that there was a chain between the Lord and Lady. This will tell us about the connection between George and this woman. They will belong to the same social set (Moon) and likely share the same professional drive for success (Moon, Sun, Heart). Basically, they will be people who love and desire the same things.

George shook his head when I told him about this woman, dismissing it as being too good to be true. Nevertheless, he asked me to describe the woman. We can do this by looking at the cards directly touching the Lady. Both the Bouquet and the Lily showed she was at least the same age or slightly younger than George. Both the Lily and the Bouquet indicated she would be fair while the Lily showed she would be voluptuous, and the Heart showed that she would be well-spoken.

Home life:

The cards for home life are the Lily and the House, showing your kin and your domestic life, respectively. The Child is your children and the Storks denote changes in the hearth. Look out for the Birds and the Storks near the Child and the House, respectively, as they show a pregnancy or a change in living arrangements.

From the domestic point of view, George's (Lord) home life (House) will be affected by his joining a new community (Garden) that will necessitate he relocates (Storks) some distance (Ship). The House mirroring the Mountain shows George has lived in his current home some time. The move is required because of a positive development in his professional life (House knighting to Stars and Moon).

The House also knights to the Dog, who was too near the Clouds for my liking. The Dog shows people we employ, so I advised George to be careful about the people he hires to help him move (Lord – Ship – Garden – Dog).

He will also be travelling (Ship being just one card away from the Lord) to a location (Garden) near the sea (Anchor). He has never been to this place before (Key), and he will go by aeroplane (Storks by the Ship). George told me he and several friends would be travelling to Phuket in Thailand at the end of the following month.

In connection with his kin, George has an influential role model in his life (Mountain far away and by the Lily). With the Tower to the right, this could be George's father. This person will soon be troubled (Rod) by anxious times (Paths).

Fortunately, the Bouquet by the Lily shows that George will be supported and that this will improve. He will introduce his family to his new girlfriend (Lady over Cavalier + Bouquet).

George had a chain between the Bear and the Lily. This shows issues concerning an older relative, usually the mother. His mum will have some upsetting (Birds) news (Letter), which will cause the family to rally around her (Bouquet).

Finances:

In terms of finances, the Fish shows income and the Ship shows opportunities and business enterprises. The House shows our comfort, while the Bear shows good luck and our general fortitude in a financial sense. The Anchor is a traditional business card in terms of stability in employment. The Mice shows thefts, which are often monetary, and the Coffin denotes financial loss.

In the coming months, George will experience difficulties (Cross) with financial affairs (Fish). This concerns an existing account (the Ring knights to the Tree and both are near the Fish). Sorting it out will be problematic (Clouds) and take him some time (Tree), and it is unlikely that it will be resolved to his satisfaction (Coffin below the Fish and the Letter). However, he has a secure (Key) wage (Ring over the Fish), so he will continue to receive his wages. The upset will pass (Birds), and he should have some positive news or increase in his salary (Cavalier).

Seeing the Ship touched by the Storks, the Moon and the Anchor is a clear sign that a change in George's employment will present him with the strongest way to improve his finances, yet being so near the House card we can also advise him that moving will present him with financial opportunities. He will be able to get a good price for his current apartment, and the property climate (House by the Garden) will be very good to him financially (Ship). Clearing out (Stars) any unwanted items should provide extra money, too (Ship).

George's long-term surety (Anchor) remains connected to his property (House). He will continue to invest in this form of security (Anchor knights to the Tree).

Career:

For employment we are concerned with the Moon, which shows our career and opportunities, and the Anchor, which denotes stability and goals. If the querent was self-employed or involved in trade we would also consider the Ship.

Seen directly to the Lord's right is a strong sign of improvement in George's career. George had already received a job offer prior to the reading, as signified by the Ship. He will accept this, bringing him a new contract (Ring) that formally recognises his career advancement such as through a new grade or more responsibility. This is a sure step (Key) towards his (Lord) long-term career success (Sun).

The job will bring him new contacts (Garden). Financially, he should receive more money, but with the Fish being so close to the Clouds, this will not be straightforward. But as the Moon also knights to the House, this problem will be short term. His salary and role are secure.

George's long-term career goals (Anchor) are best met through relocation (Ship). The Dog shows this will involve moving away from his familiar crowd. I advised George he could not expect loyalty to his current role to provide him with advancement (Dog is far away). He needs a fresh start and new contacts (Garden). The Fox being far away shows he is free of rivals.

Well-being:

To gauge a client's well-being, we need to look at the Tree (health), the Coffin (sickness) and the Tower (longevity). It is near-impossible to stop health messages appearing in a Grand Tableau. If you do see anything suspicious in the cards, tactfully advise your querent to seek appropriate medical attention.

In the coming few months, George will want to safeguard his health. There's a strong indication of headaches in both the Coffin by the Cross and the Tower over the Mountain – Rod.

He should pay close attention to his dietary intake (Bear) and be certain he knows exactly what is in his food (Stars), as there could be a stray ingredient (Dog) that does not agree with him. George might experience thinning in his hair (Bear – Coffin), possibly due to stress or worry.

George laughed when I told him he should watch his fingers (Letter). He could really hurt them (Cross) by carelessly (Clouds) catching them in a drawer or door (Coffin).

With this step, we have reviewed the entire Grand Tableau. In the next section I have included a work-through you might like to use to journal your Grand Tableaus. I can assure you, however experienced you are, you will always go back to a tableau with fresh eyes and see something new. Lay it. Read it. Save it. Review it.

Outcome

It has now been 13 months since I did that reading for George.

George did accept the job. His first day occurred late in the month, which caused some problems with his first month's pay. As the corners emphasised, he was initially reluctant to move doubting it was the right time in his life to do so. However, the 132-mile round trip proved to be too much. This caused some anxiety, but George's mother's health improved following hospital treatment.

George is also in a long-term relationship with a fair-haired woman, who also works in social care. I missed one thing in George's cards. He had several dates with another, dark-haired, woman prior to meeting his current partner. This did not last long and ended somewhat messily, which, in hindsight, was augured by the Birds by the Ring.

Grand Tableau Worksheet

You may find it useful to print out this worksheet to guide you through your own tableaus.

Date:
Cards dealt:

Note the cut and your impression?

What are the first three cards and what do they say?

What do the corners describe?

Now look at the last four cards – what do these predict?

What cards does your significator look at horizontally? Read them as the next month.

Read the cards around the Clouds – what problems can you expect?

Read the cards around the Heart, the Ring, the Anchor, and partner card – what can you expect in your romantic relationship?

Take a look at the cards around the House, the Child, the Storks, and the Lily – what is happening within your family and home?

Read the cards around the Fish, the House, the Bear, and the Ship – what is happening with your money?

Now look at the cards around the Moon and the Anchor – and the Ship if you are self-employed or involved in trade – what is happening in your working life?

Read the cards around the Tree, Coffin, Rod, and Tower to look at your well-being. What do they say?

Now look at the cards around the Cavalier and the Letter. What news will you hear?

What is the ninth card from the significator?

What are the thirteenth cards from the significator? What do these say?

The Past, Present and Future Grand Tableau

The past, present and future Grand Tableau now features in more texts than the traditional 'all-future' tableau. However, few authors have really demonstrated when it is most useful, i.e. to provide a detailed overview of a question or situation progressing from the past through to the future.

In the cult sci-fi show, 'Doctor Who', the title character bemoaned mankind's misconception of time being linear, an 'A to B' journey of cause and effect. He is quite right. Time is not linear. Modern physics is showing us that time is multi-dimensional and consists more of layers than a line.

In this setup, time flows 'around' the cards. Just like life, it is multi-dimensional. As most humans are impatient, a lot of people seem just to read a few 'lines', but this is just half (if that) of the story revealed by the cards. All cards should be considered. Thus, there is a lot of detail to filter. Herein lies both the difficulty and the usefulness of this variation of the Grand Tableau.

For this reason, it is best reserved for readings where you are focused on a situation, such as, why a marriage is having problems and where it is heading. So I advocate you always ask a question for this variation.

How I Read the Past, Present and Future Tableau

Let us break it down:

1. Cut the shuffled deck in two and read the bottom cards of each pile. This is a strong hint of the energy unfolding around the question.

2. Next, read the first three cards laid out. These are a message to the querent.

3. Read the four corners. As before, corners act like boundaries, showing overriding influences or topics in relation to the question.

4. I look at how the cards have fallen to discern which cards are near and which are far. I do the same for the Clouds, too.

For the next three steps, I will presume we have both the future and past sections. This will not always be the case, as I will discuss later.

5. Read the past cards, remembering the context of the question or situation asked.

6. Now, you can read the present cards.

7. Now, look at the future cards; continue to read your narrative and conclude with the last card. Note whether it is positive, neutral or negative. This hints at how matters will come to a close in the period covered, rather than a final outcome.

8. We conclude by looking at the theme cards. If you were asking about a financial situation, this would be the Ship, the Fish and the Anchor. For love, the Heart, the Ring, the Anchor (and the Lily in relation to them). Note where they fall in relation to time and proximity, what they are attended by, and so on.

Sometimes, there will also be a 'standout' string of cards or a traditional combination (such as timing) that draws your attention. Read these, too, always remembering the context; otherwise, you will go off on a tangent and muddle things for yourself.

Discerning what is 'Past' and what is 'Future'

For the past, present and future tableaus, I prefer the 9 x 4 (four rows of nine). For me, the past is represented by the cards to the left of the significator; the future is the cards to the right. Alternatively, you can use the way the significator faces. Thus, if you were reading for a woman, with the Blaue Eule, then the cards to the left of the Lady would be the future and those to the right would be the past.

Step 1:

Look at the following diagram:

		*						
*	*	Lady	*	*	*	*	*	*
		*						
		*						

Whatever is to the left of the Lady card is her past. In the above example, that would be the first two columns.

Whatever is to the right of the Lady card is her future. In the above illustration, that would be the fourth through the ninth columns.

The third column, which contains the Lady card, is what we will refer to as the present.

I have used '*' to show the four intersecting points of the axes of time. Hereafter, we will refer to these as the 'lines'.

Step 2:

Some readers just read the 'lines', but for me, that is akin to just reading the synopsis of a book. You will miss too much. But, as I discussed earlier, this is a method of reading that presents challenges – so people look for a shortcut.

However, we read it all in order to get the full story.

Thus, we do this:

C	C	D	E	E	E	E	E	E
B	B	Lady	F	F	F	F	F	F
A	A	D	G	G	G	G	G	G
A	A	D	G	G	G	G	G	G

Lines:

B is the main past. D is the present. F is the future.

A, the lower left, shows the most distant past. C is the more recent past.

E is the near future. G is the distant future.

As you can see, the lower half is always more distant, whereas above is more recent.

Step 3:

Now, to read this, we focus on our lines. Let us imagine the Letter card has fallen in the past 'line'. We know, therefore, that there has been a telephone call, letter, email, et cetera in the past. But we need more information.

```
    2           C          3
    B         Letter       D
    1           A          4
```

For brevity, I am going to pretend that there is only one card above or below the Letter. However, if there were two cards below and one above, you would read them as I describe here: i.e. the two cards in position C are read together under what position C signifies. At times, you will not have any cards below or above; in that case, you simply omit that position's significance.

The card in position A will tell us the Letter's most distant past, its point of origin. If the Fish were here, we could suppose finances or money were involved.

The card in position B will tell us the immediate past of the Letter. Imagine the Birds were here; we could say that financial (Fish) worries (Birds) caused someone to get in touch (Letter).

The card in position C will tell us what happened more recently, on receipt of the communication. If the Rod were here, we could say that financial (Fish) worries (Birds) caused someone to get in touch with the querent (Letter), which caused some discussions or upset (Rod).

The card in position D will tell us the outcome or conclusion of the Letter. Therefore, if the Lady card were here, we could say that financial (Fish) worries (Birds) caused someone to telephone the querent (Letter), which caused some trouble or heated discussions (Rod) between the querent and a woman (Lady).

Obviously, depending on how the cards have fallen, you could have three cards in position C (being above the letter), and none in position A. In that case, the most distant past we can read would be the immediate past (represented by B). I have found when that happens it means the most important events are more recent (as shown by position C). Similarly, when there are two or more cards in position A, we're dealing with 'old' issues.

Now, you are probably wondering what the cards in positions 1 to 4 signify. These are the linking cards. So, the card in position 1 is how A got to B, and the card in position 2 is how B links to C and so on.

	2	Rod	3
	Birds	Letter	Lady
	Coffin	Fish	4

If the Coffin were in position 1, we could say that a financial (Fish) loss (Coffin) caused the upset (Birds), which precipitated someone calling the querent (Letter), which caused some discussions or upset (Rod) between him and a woman (Lady).

As you can imagine, the card in point 4 is very important. It will represent the point of transfer; what links D to the 'next' section of past and the present.

By this point, you can see how time is moving 'around' the past cards, clockwise starting from below.

Step 4:

The present will be just one column but is supplemented by the cards to the left and right. I read these from the bottom to the top.

Cards below the querent's card tend to be events materialised in the last seven to ten days. They're often what the clients are busying themselves with or reflecting on. It is the ground they currently walk on.

Any cards above the querent's are normally what you can expect in the next seven to ten days. They are what will shortly influence events, the cliff-hanger to the next chapter.

Step 5:

We now reach the future. We do much the same with the future cards as we do the past. Only, as the lower right shows the distant future, not the past, we approach the narrative in a different order. We will pretend, again, that the Letter is our key card. So we know there is a telephone call in the future.

```
        2           B           3
        A         Letter        C
        1           D           4
```

In this case, the card in position A shows what will happen in the future that causes the telephone call to be made (Letter).

Card B tells us what will occur next, how the story develops when the Letter appears.

Whatever is in position C will indicate where this will go next.

The card in position D indicates where the dust will settle on this matter.

Again, the diagonal cards (1 thru 4) are links. The card in position 1 will show how the previous section (be it present or earlier future) got to card A. Position 2 links cards A and B together, and position 3 links cards B and A together.

Card 4 will show the end point, either of that section of the future or the end of the tableau.

Important Information

How much past and how much future is shown? The past mirrors the future. If you choose six months, then six months of the past is shown.

If the client's card is on the far left, most of the cards will show future events. This normally indicates that the client is in a very forward state of mind.

Should the card appear on the far right, this indicates quite a few ties with the past. Quite often, these clients appear to be a little restless and are not getting far quickly. The reason is often revealed in those cards.

What happens if there are no past cards or future cards? From time to time, the cards will fall so that there is either no past shown or no future. This has significance.

If there are no past cards, it shows that the querent is embarking on a new chapter. The situation you are reading is entering a whole new phase, one that will change significantly. If the querent's card happens to fall in a corner card, this is because of an action he or she is taking.

If, however, there is no future shown, this means that a chapter is about to close, and the actions the querent takes now are going to exert great weight on how the future unfolds. These tableaus very often show a great deal of causality, so examine the past very carefully to understand fully how things have unfolded. A clearer understanding will give the querent great knowledge of how best to conclude this chapter of his or her life.

Do you start over if this happens? No! You have made the decision to do a past, present and future reading. You knew that was a possibility. The cards have responded. If they have fallen so there is no past or no future, it is for a reason. It is part of the answer.

Example Reading

Zara, who is a legal secretary, came to see me in May 2014. She told me she wanted a reading on her love life. At the time, she had recently ended a four-and-a-half year relationship with Robert. They had been living together but were not married. She was finding the break up very difficult but desperately wanted to know if she had made the right decision, and if things would improve.

Focusing on her question, I spread the cards in the past, present and future tableau to look at the last and the next six months.

The cards as they fell:

Step One

When I cut Zara's cards, I received: Letter – Lily.

This shows that Zara is concerned with finding real happiness in a relationship, rather than something superficial or fleeting. There is also important news on its way concerning this.

Step Two

Now for the first three cards.

Book – House – Paths

Zara has some unexpected choices in her personal and home life now. Some options in her personal life will soon, if they have not already done so, present themselves, much to her surprise.

Step Three

The corners are: Book – Letter; Sun – Fox.

These four cards show, relative to her relationships, that there will be an unexpected telephone call. Zara will be suspicious of this call, even though it is positive in nature. Could her ex-partner, Robert, be set to surprise her?

When we look at all of this together, it does seem that there are some unexpected developments afoot. None, based on these, appear to be negative, although the Fox does add caution.

Step Four

Now, it is time to find Zara in the cards. As a woman, she is represented by card 29 – the Lady.

The Lady is in the sixth column and the third row. This shows that Zara's past (more cards to the left) is exerting a lot of influence (being in the third row) on her relationship situation right now.

In terms of proximity, there are three cards to the Lady's right and five to her left. This means that cards three positions away or more are far with the those being five places away the farthest. Cards one place away are very close and those two places away are near.

The Clouds are in the first column. The Bear, the Scythe, the Lord, the Cross and the Fox are all clouded.

Step Five

The past:

Zara's main past line starts with the Clouds. We step into this tableau through problems and confusion. There can be no greater sign that Zara's relationship sustained serious difficulties. These problems (Clouds) were caused by lies and past deceit, which caused Zara and her partner to take the wrong course (Fox). This fuelled trust issues (Bear with Fox) creating an unhealthy atmosphere full of jealousy, possessiveness and mistrust (Book and Fox mirroring each other).

It comes as little surprise that Robert was the wrong (Fox) man (Lord) for Zara. He had experienced pain (Cross) in his past due to lies (Fox). It left him with serious trust issues (Fox + Clouds) that made him very difficult and possibly aggressive whenever he felt threatened (Scythe + Snake over the Lord). He was very difficult to live with (House + Scythe). Zara felt constricted by him (Scythe + Snake).

There was no clean break, but rather a painfully slow break up (the Mice falling after the Cross) with lots of arguments instigated by Robert's attitude. These were not small spats but were volatile (Whips). We can infer that Zara was frightened and threatened by this situation (Scythe + Whips). Zara struggled to find a way out of this; she felt trapped (House + Snake). There was no support – in Zara's eyes – and her options seemed to be stacked against her (Snake + Paths).

As the relationship drew to a close, there was a lot of stress (Birds) caused by a financial loss (Mice + Coffin). Zara had to walk away empty-handed (Coffin) and was still upset (Birds) over the separation (Tower). No matter how hard she tries, she has not, thus far, been able to recoup her loss or move away from this upset (Whips + Birds). She's found several small complications and restrictions (Snake + Child) arising from the break up. This has been causing long-standing (Tower) trust issues (Snake + Child with Tower). She's also pushing away people who care for her (Child over the Birds).

Happily, there has been a small improvement recently (Clover). This is helping her overcome her personal demons and problems (Mountain below the Clover). Zara is not as lonely or isolated anymore (Clover crowning the Mountain). She is mixing with people who care for her (Clover + Child). This is making her feel, slowly but surely, a lot better (Heart) about the end of her relationship (Ring being to her left). She is now prioritising her own life and what she wants from it (Heart and Ring with the Tower).

Step Six

The present:

In the last week, Zara has made a concerted effort to move away (Ship) from her problems and negative influences (Mountain). With the Ship below her, Zara is interested in what opportunities are available to her. She wants to know how to improve her finances so that she can be more independent. This is as a direct result of the financial problems she faced at the end of her relationship (Ship following Coffin – Mountain).

She is soon to travel (if she has not already) with good friends (Clover) to a nice place (Ship – Garden).

In the coming weeks, Zara will successfully increase her financial security (Key and Fish). She will receive money from her past relationship with Robert (Fish + Ring). This will make her feel a lot better (Heart near the Fish and Key) and able to move forward.

Step Seven

The future:

Zara's future has rich developments coming in her social life (Garden near Fish). She will remain quite selective in who she mixes with (Lady before Garden) but not so isolated (Dog knights to the Lady). She will be looking for somewhere new to live (Storks below Garden). This will lead to changes that improve her health, which has suffered recently (Tree near Lady and mirroring Snake and Whips). She will join a gym (Tree over the Garden) at the advice of a doctor (Dog + Tree).

As a result of this improvement in her social life, there are developments in the shape of a man (Cavalier). As it's the Cavalier, she has not met him yet but as he knights to the Dog, he is likely known or to be met through an associate. He is young, fit, attractive (Lily), and widely respected with a very good social life (Moon). He is rooted and healthy (Key + Tree). So, it's possible she will meet him through a gym. He will prove to be stabilising for Zara, and he is the man she is hoping for (Anchor).

Zara will find that her day-to-day life improves and that she is far happier (Bouquet) as a result of this development (Bouquet). He will ask her on a date (Cavalier – Bouquet). He will behave like a perfect gentleman (Dog – Lily – Bouquet), bringing her into a luckier and more successful phase of her life (Sun – Stars). News she has been waiting to hear will arrive, too (Letter). The Letter, being the final card, emphasises this will be during the early days (as it's a neutral card), but she will find that things have improved.

Step Eight

Theme Cards:

We have read the main 'narrative' behind Zara's love life. However, we must now examine the key relationship cards: the Heart, the Ring and the Anchor. For Zara the Lord and the Cavalier are important, as they will show Robert and any future love-interest, respectively. We covered these above. The Lily should be considered in this, too.

Ring:

The Ring is both above and to the left of the Lady and near it. From this, we can infer that the recent end (it is to the left and thus, obviously, in the 'past' section) of a relationship has exerted a lot of influence over her life.

Since the Ring mirrors the Mountain, this was a problematic connection that literally tied her to Robert, who was, for Zara, closer to an enemy than a lover.

The Ring knights to the Tree, showing an unhealthy relationship, which is still affecting Zara's well-being (Tree is in the future). It also knights to the Snake (in the past), showing betrayal, and the Birds (also in the past), showing sorrow.

The boundaries show a connection to someone Zara trusted and thought highly of (Child) on a very deep level (Fish). However, these feelings were not so deep (Child + Fish) for Robert. It was also a serious relationship with joint assets and financial ties.

Ultimately, the lack of mutual love (Heart) meant it was not going to last (Tower). However, there is a future relationship to come (Key). This relationship will involve someone who loves Zara deeply (Child – Heart – Fish). The Ring being so close, knighting to the Lady, emphasises this, too.

Heart:

The Heart is to the left and one position away from the Lady. This shows both Zara's desire for love and her recent heartache.

The Clover is mirrored from the Heart, meaning she loves to be surrounded by people, and the simple joys of a relationship bring her happiness.

The boundaries show she has recently experienced sorrow in love (Birds). For her, being in love is the key to long-term happiness; she does not see her future as being single (Tower).

There is new love coming (Key) for her (Lady). This will be a love of deep and rich feelings (Fish). Knighting from the Heart also confirms that this new love is connected through a friend's social contacts (Dog and Garden).

Anchor:

The Anchor has fallen to the lower right of the Lady. It is touched by positive cards and one neutral card. This is a strong sign that Zara's hopes in love will be satisfied.

It mirrors the House, the Cross and the Moon. From this, we can see that previously Zara had a grounded, secure and fairly traditional relationship with shared assets (House). She was very heavily invested in this partnership and worked on it a lot (Moon). When this ended, it caused her a lot of pain (Cross).

What do the Anchor's boundaries and clusters show us? The Garden and the Bouquet talk about her social life and hobbies. However, the Bouquet is directly over the Letter. To me, this shows that changes will occur when she is invited over the telephone to a social event where she will be introduced to someone. Who will she meet? The Cavalier, who is crowned by the Lily, indicating that he will bring her happiness. I thus had to remedy my earlier statement of meeting him at the gym. This happiness is in the shape of her hopes for changes (Storks + Anchor).

The Anchor knights to the Lady, the Tree and the Stars, bringing luck to her long-term wishes and steady improvement in her health issues.

Standout Combinations:

Zara had several standout combinations; however, the one I wish to show you is the celestial cards. That is the Stars, the Sun and the Moon cards. Whenever these cards fall together and close to the significator, it is an auspicious sign of improvement, growth and protection. Protection is also emphasised by the Lily touching each one of these cards.

In this context, Zara wanted a love that will bring happiness (Lily), respect (Moon), growth (Sun) and improvement to her life (Stars). She had not found it with Robert but she will with someone new. They will prove a protective influence for her.

Outcome

I am very happy to report that Zara's reading played out as the cards showed. She is now very happy in a new relationship and has taken up equestrian sports! Her ex-partner, Robert, also agreed to a financial settlement, which surprised her greatly.

Fan Spreads

Fans, or line spreads, are my personal favourites for answering quick questions. I am a big believer in questions. Questions give us context and prevent us from falling into supposition. I do not often use the Grand Tableau for quick questions because I do not always need that level of detail.

Instead, I deal a certain number of cards into a row. As hinted at above, the number depends on the detail I need. The following table should give you an idea.

3 cards – daily readings, yes-or-no questions – minimum level of detail.

5 cards – quick questions, yes-or-no with explanation – clear answer with the bare bones.

7 cards – two-part questions – basic answer with some detail.

9 cards – any question – full answer with lots of details.

I rarely do seven-card deals as most of my clients' questions, and my own, fall into the five- or nine-card category in terms of detail needed. If I needed more than nine cards I would use the Grand Tableau. For this reason only three-, five- and nine-card spreads are dealt with hereafter. I then cover the 3 x 3 which is made up of three fans of three.

Daily Readings

Daily readings are a good way to become familiar with the Petit Lenormand. People new to the system find them a challenge, as the cards' meanings exist on a spectrum of weight.

In a daily reading, cards will carry the lightest form of their meaning 98% of the time. For instance, the Clouds is more likely to show it is going to be foggy or raining, and at worst one of those days when things do not go to plan, rather than severe misfortune or trouble. If you see the Coffin it usually means a headache, or even something to do with refuse. Cards like the Sun or Stars might point to specific times, morning or night, respectively.

For daily draws to be worthwhile you need to be in the right frame of mind to realise that Clouds – Fox – Coffin may well mean having to pick up litter because next door's cat has ripped open the bin bags, rather than being defrauded and left in penury. The cards are often literal, and can even tell you the weather.

It is also best to do your daily draws on the day itself. I do not know why, although I expect it is something to do with our minds' processing, but doing a daily draw on the night before often ends up being a summary of the preceding day.

Similarly, be careful of your question. 'What is happening to ME today?' is not the same as 'What is happening today?' I advise you to use the former.

My personal preference in reading daily draws is to take the first card as the main topic of the day. The Letter here would most likely mean a telephone call, letter or the newspaper. Cards two and three tell you about the topic.

Here are a couple of examples:

I pulled these cards on 29 January 2014.

Lord – Scythe – Bear

These cards stumped me at the time. But they predicted that I (Lord) would cut myself (Scythe) whilst shaving (the Bear represents hair, including facial hair).

I pulled these on 2 March 2014.

Dog – Paths – Garden

Since I have pet dogs, the Dog signifies them. I had to take my dogs (Dog) the long way to the park (Garden) because of road diversions (Paths).

Exercise #4 – Daily Draws

For the next month (or week, at minimum), deal yourself three cards each morning. Record the cards you dealt, your summarisation of their meaning, and make sure you predict an event! At the end of each day record how accurate you were.

Be honest.

Yes or No

Basic yes-or-no questions are quite easy with the Petit Lenormand. What you do is ask a question and deal off three cards, then read them based on whether they are positive, positive-neutral, neutral, neutral-negative, or negative. This confuses some people. Imagine you ask, 'Will my boyfriend end our relationship?' You get three negatives, the answer is 'no' he will not dump you. Three positives, yes he will.

You do have to allow for a 'maybe' answer if you happen to pull three neutral cards. Experience has taught me that it is more often a 'maybe not' rather than a positive 'maybe'. Similarly, two neutrals tend to take the flavour of the third card – be it positive (likely yes) or negative (likely no).

If you want to know why the answer has come back as yes or no, read the cards' meanings. Here are two genuine examples.

Henry, a cardiac nurse, wanted to know if Joseph loved him. Does X love me? is a question I see a lot, and as long as you are clear on whether it is romantic or platonic love, the cards will answer you clearly enough.

Cross – Book – Lady

The Cross is negative and the Book is neutral-negative, whereas the Lady is null. The answer is no, Joseph does not love Henry. Why? He is about to (Cross) meet a new (Book) woman (Lady). Henry soon found out Joseph was not gay.

My guilty pleasure is an occasional flutter. Before I ventured to the local shop for my newspaper in December 2013, I asked the cards if I would be lucky that day (it was the Euro millions draw that night!).

Letter – Fish – Stars

The Letter is neutral, and the Fish and Stars are both positive. As Letter – Fish is often a bank statement or cheque I purchased a scratch card rather than a lottery ticket (which I see as Letter – Clover), and was lucky making the glorious sum of £3 on my £2 purchase.

Lines of Five

Five cards will give you a succinct answer to a clear question, with more detail than a simple yes-or-no draw. This is my go-to spread for questions I have on a day-to-day basis or when I need to know where I stand with a problem or issue.

If you have a two-parted question, I suggest you break it up. 'Am I going to lose my job and will I find another one?', is two questions. That's two lines of five.

To create a line of five, simply deal out five cards in a row. I like odd numbers for line spreads because they produce a hinge card, which is useful in spreads of five or more cards. I always look at the middle card first in a line of five, seven, or nine. It provides a theme or general focus for the reading.

You can then read the cards straight across, going left to right. If you need any extra detail you can mirror cards one and five, as well as cards two and four.

While you can preselect the middle card, or use a variation of the 'Opening of the Key Spread', I feel it reduces the spread to two 2-card readings. If you do this, I suggest you read the first two cards together and then the last two cards together as a past and future spread.

Rebecca's question was, *'What does Ross think of me romantically?'*

Birds – Lady – Dog – Child – Garden

The middle card shows Ross is friendly towards Rebecca. However, he is set to bring Rebecca some disappointment (Birds) as Ross only sees her (Lady) as a friend (Dog) he likes and thinks well of (Child) in his circle (Garden). The Garden, being more than two cards away from the Lady, shows that this is not going to be enough, or right, for Rebecca. There won't be a romantic relationship. This will make her feel sad and let down for a time (Birds – Garden), but she has people who will help her through it (Lady – Child).

For a second example, Ben asked me, *'What is stopping me getting a job?'*

Mice – Ship – Book – Lily – Garden

The Book in the middle of the line most likely represents Ben's education or skill base. As we're concerned with what is stopping Ben getting a job, this position means it is an issue. He's losing out (Mice) on opportunities (Ship) because of his education or lack of skills (Book), which is stopping him find an entry job (Lily – Garden). The last two cards point to Ben needing help from a project (Book) mentor or patron (Lily) to meet people (Garden) in an appropriate workplace.

Ben has dyslexia and went on a skills placement organised by Connexions, an outreach programme in the UK, something the Lily can signify.

Lines of Nine

The line of nine is my favourite spread when I need a clear and detailed response. It is also good for two-parted questions, or when you want a reading to cover or predict outcomes for eight to twelve weeks' time. You can preselect a topic card (i.e., Fish for money) and place it in position five if you wish, but I seldom ever do.

Once you have dealt your nine cards in a row, look at card five for a focus. Then read the cards left to right as an answer. You can mirror cards for extra detail if you wish. Cards one and nine mirror each other, as do cards two and eight, and cards three and seven.

Grace asked me for a line of nine about her love life. Her question was, *'What is happening to me in love?'*

Dog – Ring – Snake – Clouds – Heart – Lady – Moon – Lord – Bouquet

The first thing to note is that the Lady card, which stands for Grace, has appeared. Both the Lord and the Dog appear, so we have two men. The Ring has fallen to the left of the Lady, and even though this is not a Grand Tableau, I still note this as significant. We are, after all, dealing with love. If we look at the suits hearts (the Dog, the Heart, the Moon, the Lord) and clubs (the Ring, the Snake, the Clouds) dominate. From this we infer that he love will trouble her but ending on a spades card (the Bouquet) promises betterment.

There is a man in Grace's life (Dog) that she has strong ties to (Ring) which are set to unravel (Snake – Clouds). Dog – Bouquet implies that this was a happy connection in its time. With the Dog falling at some distance to the Lady, it indicates that this was not a serious relationship (at least not for all parties), and this will be putting the squeezers on Grace's heartstrings.

Unfortunately, this is going to prove quite a bad and complicated affair (Ring – Snake). Grace will find out that this man is not interested in her, and that he is actually interested in another woman (Snake is the Queen of Clubs). As the Snake is mirroring the Moon this could be a female work colleague. I'd say, based on experience, with the Moon present it is at least a woman known to the querent. This will cause Grace a lot of upset and pain (Clouds) and fuel a sense of betrayal (Snake – Clouds – Heart).

Clouds – Heart – Lady shows a sense misfortune in love that will take Grace some time to get over. The Clouds is to the left of the Lady and the Heart, so this will not be as bad as it could be, but this is cold comfort. She will still feel pretty rough, but might escape the worst of it.

Grace does have another man interested in her. The Moon is chained by the Lady and the Lord, so this is a more admirable and upright (Moon) chap (Lord) and a connection that is set to bring her a lot more happiness. He will be someone who has a stable job, good reputation, and is probably quite good looking in a classical sense (Moon – Lord). This relationship will bring her a lot more happiness (Bouquet), but he will want to start off slowly.

As the Ring is to the left, and the Anchor has not presented itself, I cannot say this is the real deal. She will at least, I expect, find this helps her to get over the other chap (Dog).

After doing this reading, Grace told me that there was a man with whom she had an on-and-off thing, but he did not seem to want to commit and she suspected that he was interested in another woman. She was hoping the cards would indicate he'd do a U-turn. I told her if this was the case she should walk away now as that might save a lot of heartache (Clouds). A few weeks on, Grace told me she had done just that, and her ex was now seeing someone else. It still hurt her, but she was optimistic about the future.

The following line of nine is one I did for myself in January 2014. Because of ill-health and government cutbacks resulting in the loss of a fixed-term contract I held, I had suffered some financial difficulties. I asked the cards, *'Will this situation improve and how?'*

Cross – Lord – Ring – Fish – Birds – Letter – Ship – Cavalier – Sun

There was no real dominance of one suit but three diamonds echoed the precarious nature of my question. The middle card is the Birds, and being more than two cards away from the Lord, I took it as anxieties rather than sorrow. So I could expect some financial anxieties for a while. Quite often the Birds' worries are related to everyday life, which is affected by a change in one's financial status.

Cross – Lord showed that I (Lord) could expect some hardship (Cross) in my financial situation in the near future, and I couldn't do much to avoid this. That the Cross fell next to my card did, however, mean that it would not last forever and that I (Lord after the Cross) was past the worst of it. The Sun mirroring the Cross, and at distance from the Lord, showed that the problems were because of disappointing (Sun) events (Cross). As the Sun is so far away, it can also mean feeling cold.

However, I (Lord) had a chance of new contracts (Ring) in business (Fish), which would potentially generate lucrative sources of income (Ring – Fish). These dealings (Ring) would yield new opportunities, too (Ship).

Fish – Birds – Letter talks about news that causes upset over finances, specifically concerning two (Birds) sources of income (Fish). In this case it spelled out a loss of one of the two. This would be flagged up in financial statements (Fish – Letter) concerning business contracts (Ring – Ship). But I should have some news from overseas (Cavalier being far away and by the Ship) which would help (Cavalier – Sun).

The cards were right. I did indeed lose my one day a week role, but I have slowly been able to recover some of that lost money. It was hard work (Cross), and I did indeed have problems with heating my home, but I suddenly received more e-mail readings from clients all across the world, and I also received a proposal from Europe to author some literature.

3 x 3

As the name suggests, the 3 x 3, also called the square of nine or box spread, is a layout that uses three rows of three cards. Thus we are really reading three horizontal and vertical fans and two diagonal fans. This is an important factor to be considered in terms of scope and timing.

I have found that the Grand Tableau often discusses the present and events taking place in approximately twelve weeks' time. I use three cards for daily draws. Based on this ratio of cards to timeframes, I have found the 3 x 3 is best to review a question, or your life in general, for over the next two to four weeks.

What this spread has in its favour when compared to others is its layout allows for crowning (vertical attendance). The cards in the first row can be seen as influencing those in the middle and bottom rows.

Considering this, you should remember that the cards' meanings will not be quite as heavy, or as full as they would be in a reading covering three months to year, but they will be heavier than in a daily reading. As a rule this is most important when dealing with the Clouds card and any card that is clouded.

The 3 x 3 is a well-known and widely used layout, popular with a variety of decks, such as the tarot or Petit Etteilla. For this reason alone, there are numerous methods of reading it. Here I document the version I use professionally as of April 2015, although I have used many others.

Reading the 3 x 3

1. Lay out the cards top to bottom, as shown below.

$$1-2-3$$
$$4-5-6$$
$$7-8-9$$

2. Check for dominance of both suits and either positive or negative cards, remembering how cards can become negative with other cards (like the Clover or the Stars with the Clouds). More negative cards, or Clubs, signify a challenging few weeks or trouble connected to the question.

3. In any spread that uses more than five cards, I always expect to see at least one card that relates to the question or area of focus. If one has not appeared it is often a sign that the area being asked about is not the prime concern or that other areas are affecting it.

4. Read card 5, shown below, as the main theme or atmosphere for the coming weeks. Some readers preselect this card if they wish to focus on an area such as money (Fish) or health (Tree), but I prefer to let it fall randomly.

Then read the four corners (1 - 3 and 7 - 9) as card five's boundaries to see what the overriding influences will be.

5. Finally, you can now read the cards in rows of three: 1 - 2 - 3; 4 - 5 - 6; 7 - 8 - 9; 1 - 4 - 7; 2 - 5 - 8; 3 - 6 - 9. You can then read the diagonals, 1 - 5 - 9 and 3 - 5 - 7. I often read the first row with the first column and so on. For clarity and illustrative purposes I have not done so here. When you read the fans, remember the rules of vertical attendance.

I find this exhausts the cards and gives a decent, albeit not in-depth, preview of the next few weeks.

Distance

Distance from the significator and the Clouds matters quite a lot in a 3 x 3 for finding the right meanings to derive combinations.

$$1-2-3$$
$$4-5-6$$
$$7-8-9$$

Return to the illustration of how to lay out the 3 x 3 above. If we take the first card as our hypothetical significator, cards 2, 4 and 5 are very near. Cards 3, 6, 7, 8 and 9 are far, being three positions from card 1.

At the time of writing I utilise a very strict approach with the 3 x 3. Due to its structure, a card one place away from the significator or the Clouds cards is always near, and anything further is far. I no longer use middle meanings unless neither the significator or Clouds appears, in which case all cards are treated as being neither near nor far.

Example 1

Auglefo is a second year university student. She came to see me in March 2015 following a recommendation from a friend who is a regular client of mine. Auglefo was a doing well in her studies, but said she felt a bit disenchanted and bored with the current tide of her life. Her question was, 'What can I expect in the coming weeks?'

Step One:

I shuffled, cut and dealt Auglefo's cards:

Birds – Heart – Paths
Bear – Stars – Lord
Bouquet – Dog – Child

Neither the Lady card nor the Clouds card has appeared, thus all cards take their middle meaning.

Step Two:

Auglefo had drawn two cards from Diamonds (Birds, Paths), two from Spades (Bouquet, Child) and one from Clubs (Bear). There were four cards from Hearts (Heart, Stars, Lord and Dog).

Hearts primarily represent our day-to-day life and domestic affairs. Combined with Diamonds (precarious nature of life and changes) and Spades (happiness, growth in our lives and important relationships with other people) we can infer that in her daily affairs (Hearts) Auglefo has some changes (Diamonds) bringing growth and happiness (Spades) to look forward to. The one Clubs card would say that these are not without some hiccups.

In terms of positivity there are three positive cards (Bouquet, Stars and Heart) and two positive-neutral cards (Child and Dog). There are two neutral cards (Bear and Paths) and one neutral-negative card (Birds). As positive cards dominate – and with there being no overly negative cards – Auglefo's cards showed an overall pleasant and content time.

Step Three:

Auglefo's question is somewhat subjective and does not relate to a specific theme, such as finances or love. Nevertheless I was pleased to see the Bouquet and the Stars present and the dominance of Hearts cards. I felt these promised improvement to her sense of disenchantment, while also connecting to her question of what to look forward to, being and hopeful 'improvement' cards.

Step Four:

Card 5 is the Stars. Having the Stars here promises that Auglefo can expect some improvement in life. Considering what she told me beforehand, and how the Stars can represent the human psyche, I also said that she should be thinking and feeling clearer about her life and this should make her feel happier.

The Stars' four boundary cards were the Birds, the Paths, the Bouquet and the Child. It is worth recalling that the Birds and the Paths lie above the Stars; they are influencing the Stars. Worry and stress about a decision (Birds – Paths) in the coming weeks can easily trouble the mind (Stars); however, the worries will pass when a decision is made and as always with the Paths, Auglefo should use her initiative and all things will right themselves (Stars). That is something to look forward to, as are some pleasant times with someone who cares about her (Bouquet – Child).

Step Five:

Now we will read the fans, starting with the three rows and then the columns and end with the diagonals. I have to keep this very compartmentalised for clarity's sake. You should be able to see why I prefer to read the first row with the first column, and so on, as they invariably relate to each other due to sharing the same first card.

You will have noticed that card 28, the Lord, appeared in Auglefo's reading. I told her that this will be the most significant man in her life, such as a boyfriend. She replied, somewhat coyly, that there was no one at that time.

Birds – Heart – Paths: In the next few weeks Auglefo will have to make a decision about a matter that makes her feel anxious in its uncertainty. However, once made, she could look forward to feeling more in control.

Bear – Stars – Lord: Auglefo can expect dealings with a man who possess a great intellectual prowess that has earned him some clout (the Bear preceding the Stars shows good fortune or power through intelligence).

Bouquet – Dog – Child: Auglefo can expect a new chapter to begin with a pleasant friend who thinks well of her.

Birds – Bear – Bouquet: Auglefo will experience significant anxiety and worry (Birds – Bear) but there will be someone there who can offer her attention and protection (Bear – Bouquet). As the Dog touches both the Bouquet and the Bear I told Auglefo this would be the friend rather than the Lord.

Heart – Stars – Dog: Heart – Stars traditionally harbours strong love (some romantics might say love at first sight, especially when they fall with the Bouquet between the significator and partner cards). With the Dog here we can say that Auglefo can expect a successful development in love with someone she can trust.

Paths – Lord – Child: Auglefo can expect to make a choice regarding a man who thinks well of her.

Now we can look at the diagonals.

Birds – Stars – Child: Following some anxiety, Auglefo can expect a successful new start and an improvement.

Paths – Stars – Bouquet: Auglefo can expect a new perspective which will allow her to make the right decision.

Outcome:

After the reading I explained to Auglefo that I felt the Lord and the Dog were two men she had romantic feelings for. The Dog was someone she knew and might have already dated, whereas the Lord was the person she was more interested in. She advised me she was concerned with this and that this is the reason she was feeling somewhat disillusioned.

I told her she would make a choice within the next few weeks about this matter but the cards pointed to the Dog offering her a new start and sincere affection. Once the choice was made she would feel a lot better and more optimistic.

I heard from Auglefo in May when she booked a Grand Tableau. She is now back with her ex-partner, the Dog, but remains good friends with the Lord who is helping her with her studies.

Example 2

Cynthia booked a reading with me via my website. She lived in the state of Mississippi and was finding it difficult to cope at home. Her two teenaged sons were constantly fighting and were causing conflict between Cynthia and her husband. She asked, 'Why are my teenagers always fighting?'

I shuffled and cut and dealt a 3 x 3 for her.

Step One:

I dealt Cynthia's cards as follows:

House – Birds – Mountain
Garden – Key – Dog
Fox – Bouquet – Rod

Once again neither the Lady nor the Clouds has appeared; thus all cards take their middle meaning. Interestingly, the Child (Cynthia's children) did not appear. This shows that the children themselves will not take an active part in solving matters.

Step Two:

Cynthia has three cards from Clubs, which is the most difficult suit and shows a lot of problems. There are two cards from Hearts (domestic), Diamonds (cares and concerns) and Spades (happiness) so these are affecting (Diamonds) the household's (Heart) happiness (Spades).

The Mountain, the Rod, the Fox and the Birds are all in negative positions showing that this is a problematic and difficult time; however, the presence of the Key does show a solution can be found.

Step Three:

The Rod, the card of strife and quarrels, has appeared reinforcing the question. Also we have both the Key (domestic and home life) and the Birds (upsets and grief). These reinforce Cynthia's question and highlight it as an issue (Key in the middle touching the other cards).

Step Four:

The middle card was the Key. This shows there is certainly something wrong but a solution is available that will lead to improvement.

Looking at the boundaries, the reason Cynthia's children were fighting is that nobody is talking honestly about the problems at the hearth (House – Mountain – Fox – Rod).

I also looked at the inner cross (cards 2, 4, 5, 6 and 8). I find this is useful when a concrete question has been asked, and it can often describe the answer. The solution lies in seeing that there is a lot of stress and upset connected to rivalry within their peers in the neighbourhood and fitting-in (Birds – Garden – Key – Dog – Bouquet).

Step Five:

We will now look at the fans, commencing with the three rows. Once again I have to keep this very compartmentalised for clarity. In practice you can take a more fluid approach.

Carefully addressing the issue around the household as a whole is needed (House – Key – Rod), but tread carefully and develop a strategy (Mountain – Key – Fox).

House – Birds – Mountain: Right now, Cynthia's children are upset that they are not getting out of the house much but nobody is addressing the reason for this.

Garden – Key – Dog: There is an important event coming up with their peers that they want to attend.

Fox – Bouquet – Rod: Currently, they both are trying very hard to keep a civil tongue to impress Cynthia, in the hope of attending.

House – Garden – Fox: The neighbourhood has issues with rival groups where there have been previous betrayals.

Birds – Key – Bouquet: Current upset and high tension about this is passing with the promise of reconciliation, too. I told Cynthia that as the Fox knights to both the Dog and the Birds (two friends), it's clear that the children are taking rival (Fox) sides, hence their quarrels.

Mountain – Dog – Whips: Problems arising from this need to be addressed openly and honestly in order to diffuse the tension.

Synopsis:

As Cynthia had booked an email reading I included a summary based on the information I had pooled from the reading. I wrote: *'There's conflict amongst their peers which is not being acknowledged but has put them at loggerheads. Solving it will involve looking at their peer groups and healing rifts amongst their friends.'*

Outcome:

I did not hear from Cynthia until early 2015. She told me that she had found her teenagers were indeed taking sides between rival factions. Things improved only after the family decided to relocate and the children made new friends, and stress was reduced.

Pyramid Spread

The pyramid spread is one of just three layouts I use with the Petit Lenormand that has a 'shape'. Like the 3 x 3 it has the bonus of crowning cards so we can get a clear sense of cause and effect. However it differs from the 3 x 3 in that the events discussed do not occur with such immediacy.

For this reason I use it mostly when I have a question that is focused on discerning a cause or root issue and when I do not want to focus on a short time frame.

There are several variations of this spread. I use ten cards, but other readers can use between six and fifteen – even thirty-six.

I prefer to lay my cards from the bottom to top. My cousin, who lives and reads in Romania and who taught me the layout, lays the cards top to bottom.

Reading the Pyramid

Once the question is decided on, shuffle, cut and deal the cards as follows.

$$
\begin{array}{c}
10 \\
8-9 \\
5-6-7 \\
1-2-3-4
\end{array}
$$

1. I recommend turning over the levels one at a time, starting with 1 – 2 – 3 – 4. Read them first as a row of four then 1 – 4 and 2 – 3.

I find that this row gives me the core answer. For instance if you asked why you were finding it difficult to sell a product, these cards give the basic reason. The subsequent levels elaborate or add context as to why this is.

2. Now read cards 5 – 6 – 7 as a triple and then pair cards 5 and 7.

3. Now read card 5 in relation to cards 1 and 2, then card 6 with cards 2 and 3, and card 7 with cards 3 and 4. Remember the card above influences the card below.

4. Next read cards 8 and 9 together.

5. Now read card 8 with cards 5 and 6, and card 9 with cards 6 and 7.

6. Card 10 is the crowning card and provides the main influence. This should be read as directly influencing cards 8 and 9. You can also read it in conjunction with cards 1 – 5 – 8 and cards 4 – 7 – 9.

Example Reading

Michelle is a 40-year-old single woman with a busy career. She booked a reading with me in May 2014. Her question was: 'Why can I not find the right man for a serious relationship and when will this change?'

After talking the question over with her, and because Michelle wanted to know when this would change, I decided on the pyramid layout to give her the reason and why this was an issue. We also decided to focus on the reason why she was not finding the right man as opposed to when she would.

The cards as they fell:

Garden
Rod – Clover
Moon – Storks – House
Dog – Bouquet – Fox – Lord

Step One:

As to why Michelle cannot find the right man for a serious relationship, the cards point the finger at her friends! She has good friends who are trying to be helpful (Dog – Bouquet) but lead to, quite literally, the wrong man (Fox – Lord). I explained to Michelle that the cards implied her friends were setting her up with men they knew and liked (Dog – Lord) but they were not really what Michelle wanted or liked (Clover – Fox).

Michelle's response was that the last few dates she had been on were with men known to her circle of friends.

Step Two:

The next level is made up of the Moon, the Storks and the House. These state that professional changes (Moon – Storks) have affected her personal and domestic life (Storks – House), further affecting her ability to find love. Moon – House often means someone who either works from home or in property. Michelle told me she works most of the week from home, but has to go to Manchester once a week and this involves an overnight stay at the weekends.

Step Three:

Looking further we can see that Michelle's professional life is affecting her ability to spend time and find new friends and relationships (the Moon over the Dog and the Bouquet). This has meant that a lot of the changes in her relationship status have been wrong (the Storks over the Bouquet and the Fox) and has led to her inviting the wrong men into her life (the House over the Fox and the Lord).

Step Four:

Very often the Rod – Clover, without other negative cards near them, refers to short, heated discussions or minor disagreements with people. The contentious issue fizzles out quickly with little effect afterwards.

Here those cards point to the fact that Michelle has some minor annoyances or niggles that have prevented her from finding the right man. The people she has dated thus far have proved not to be 'right', much to her annoyance, although they have not parted on bad terms per se.

Step Five:

Seeing the Rod over the Moon – Storks cards is indicative of a lot of strife causing changes in her professional life and affecting Michelle on a day-to-day basis (both the Moon and the Storks cards are from the suit of Hearts). Chances are these difficulties have caused some displacement within her personal coteries (Moon – Storks).

As the Clover follows the Rod we need to consider that it could point to brief disagreements with the people Michelle used to socialise or draw comfort from. This has resulted in changes on a personal level (Clover over the Storks – House).

Step Six:

The final card is the Garden. In terms of what is stopping Michelle from finding love, she is not really going to places where she can meet like-minded people who she can feel comfortable with. This has been a trend running through the cards and the Garden is the final confirmation. Michelle needed to get out there and mix.

Interestingly, the Garden with the Rod can point to public debates or simply a place where people can go and talk, often about issues they are passionate about. While the Garden – Clover can be places where people 'get lucky' (or just find luck, context counts).

This is further referenced on the left side of the pyramid: Dog – Moon – Rod – Garden. A friendly place with a good reputation where people can go, in the evening (Moon = evening), to talk.

I advised Michelle to look for singles' nights that were centred on interests she had and felt passionate about.

Timing:

Michelle had also asked when things would change. There was no specific timeframe set in the question, and no combination that overwhelmingly pointed to a timeframe.

In a spread that does not use all the cards, if the significator has not appeared you can go through the remaining pack and see what card the significator faces. Excluding the four Aces (as the significator will always be either the Lady (Ace of Spades) or the Lord (Ace of Hearts)), the remaining cards can be associated with a timeframe (see appendix 4).

In my deck the Lady faced right. When I found her she was looking at card 12, the Birds. The Birds is the 7 of Diamonds. Diamonds is associated with the summer season, and each card roughly corresponds to ten days. The Bird can thus be seen as being up to 22 days after the start of summer.

So Michelle should have some improvement in her love life by 13 July.

Outcome:

I read for Michelle again in November 2014. She did indeed meet someone in early summer at a gardening exhibition held in Birmingham. Although the relationship has not lasted (as mentioned above, we did not read on when Mr Right would appear), it was the start of improvement in both her love and social life.

Conclusion

This concludes our review of the Petit Lenormand method. As I said earlier, this is an introduction. It's also not the only way. My hope is that it has dispelled some myths and whetted your appetite to learn more about traditional fortune-telling practices with these cards.

As you have seen, the traditional method is neither complicated nor rigid. It is linguistic and employs much the same techniques as 19th century stenographic and shorthand systems, like Pitman. Rather than being above, on or below lines, we use near and far.

Simplicity is the method's strength. It does not need to be reinvented, because it is easily adaptable to our lives (like having the Letter stand for faxes and emails). Do not be fooled, however, that there is no difference between using the method and just using the cards. There is.

A good example of this is how the Petit Lenormand is used by many readers as an aid to practices such as Vodou, Santería and Hoodoo in the USA or Candomblé in Brazil. These practitioners largely still use the Philippe Lenormand-derived meanings. The Fish is still wealth and the ocean, and because of that, it is associated with the ocean, the Orisha Yemaya or the Lwa La Sirène. Because the Clover shows our desire for happiness and can show herbs and vegetables, it often signifies that the client may be in need of good luck and protection wanga or gris-gris made with roots and herbs.

I use the cards in similar a way in my practice of traditional farmichi (traditional Rrom folk magick practised in Eastern Europe).

We can only do this by working with the traditional meanings and watching the cards' essences unfold in our lives.

Andy Boroveshengra
Bridgnorth, United Kingdom
May 2015

Appendix #1 – Describing People

While 34 of the cards can describe a person, several can be person-cards. Where this is applicable, I've given information under the heading 'Person'.

Under the heading of 'Description', I've included personality or lifestyle characteristics and physical descriptions. Not all cards, such as the Key, give physical characteristics. Some cards such as the Cross add a physical description that can be through a uniform or attire (e.g. a nun) rather than a physiological feature.

The Lord and Lady cards simply stand for a man and woman, respectively. One will always be you or the person having the reading, and this is decided by sex. These cards do not describe anything else.

I must stress the information given here is not to be taken as an exhaustive list.

How to Use This Information:

Cards that form a 'cluster' around a person card, i.e. to the left, to the right, and above or below in a Grand Tableau, describe that person either physically or through personality or lifestyle. Look up the information given here, and you should be able to build up a profile of the person.

For example:

The Snake shows an older person with spectacles, lithe and with dark or grey hair.

The Key indicates the Dog will be important in the querent's future but doesn't add a physical description.

The Lily shows someone who is sexy, young, fair and muscular.

The Ship indicates that someone is self-employed or an entrepreneur and physically a first- or second-generation immigrant, but not accented.

We could, therefore, say this man is going to be a valuable friend (Key) in the future. He's attractive (Lily) and exotic looking (Ship) with a slim build and is at least the same age as the querent (Snake's age and Lily's youth cancel each other out) with dark blonde or brown hair (Snake + Lily) and spectacles (Snake) and whose parents or grandparents were born abroad (Ship).

MEANINGS:

1. – Cavalier.

Description: If far away, foreign or of a different ethnicity or culture to the querent. Young, well-kept, physically toned and lithe. Someone 'up-and-coming' with good prospects.

Person: A man, future male lover. Male same-sex partner.

2. – Clover.

Description: Joyful, affectionate and earthy/personable unless near the Clouds card, which indicates they are pessimistic, lonely and depressed; often physically plump with brown or copper hair and hazel/green eyes.

3. – Ship.

Description: Entrepreneurs and sales representatives, or more often self-employed – dreamer, idealist. Physically, someone who is first- or second-generation immigrant, with close ties or family abroad; often with an exotic look or different ethnicity to querent but without a foreign accent.

4. – House.

Description: Someone stable, loyal with a comfortable lifestyle and community minded – can be a local elder or head of the neighbourhood watch. Physically, someone who is older with square, broad features and a conservative dress sense.

Person: Male, same age or older than the querent. Community leader, mentor, honorary 'uncle.'

5. Tree.

Description: Dark-skinned and often middle aged. Can be of an 'old family' in the area or have an old, well-known name. Characteristics are inertia, boredom, and a habitual and ponderous manner.

6. Clouds.

Description: Someone who is very difficult and unpleasant and can be malevolent in personality. The cause of the querent's troubles. Physically, the same age to older with dark or grey hair.

Person: Older man, male ex-partner. Also male boss, etc.

7. Snake

Description: Lithe frame, dark or grey haired, often wears spectacles or contact lenses, and sometimes has a strange gait or scoliosis. Flippant in speech, intelligent and moderately voiced/lisp.

Person: Older woman, female ex-partner. Boss. Female same-sex partner.

8. Coffin.

Description: When to the right they can be musical, artistic or a designer. Otherwise, sickly, draining or hard life/bankrupt. Physically, gaunt and pale and sometimes 'Goth' or 'Emo'.

9. Bouquet.

Description: Light skin, blonde or light brown hair, often the same age or younger than the querent. Well-kept and often beautiful, expressive eyes (blue, usually). Has a very charming and pleasant but shy or quiet personality.

Person: Younger woman, adult female; a child if the querent has several grandchildren.

10. Scythe.

Description: Volatile and intimidating personality; often indicates someone has a criminal record of violent crimes. Physically scarred or tattooed (with Bouquet) body with short hair or shaved head.

With the Tree, this person would be a surgeon, dentist, etc.

11. Rod.

Description: Strong and distinctive voice (accent, stutter, etc.), talkative and can be involved with pressure groups and trade unions. Very often multilingual. Physically overbearing, sweaty and awkward. If near the Coffin card, someone who is deaf or mute and uses sign language.

12. Birds.

Description: Someone who has suffered a shock or recent upset; is sorrowful in nature and dislikes crowds. If good cards surround, then talkative or excitable. Often indiscreet and unable to keep secrets. Physically, large eyes, small features and sparrow-like build.

Person: Grandparents, aunt and uncle, or adult siblings who live together.

13. Child.

Description: Someone who loves and cares for the querent; a close, intimate friend. Physically young, with a slight build and aquiline features; typically light haired.

Person: Child or grandchildren of any gender, etc. In love questions, a woman.

14. Fox.

Description: Physically long nose and hawkish features with green eyes and red or strawberry-blonde hair. Someone who is a loner and lives away from family, often a cat fancier. Also unsociable, 'toothy', and can be a work rival or illegal worker.

Person: Rival or work colleague of either sex. In legal questions, the lawyer of the opponent.

15. Bear.

Description: Long brown or black hair, bearded if male, and can have dark skin and brown/black eyes. Broad, well-built and sturdy. Has a covetous personality, enjoys beautiful things and has a dominant figure.

Person: Older person (mother, grandmother or aunt) as well as supervisor (not a top boss).

16. Stars.

Description: Someone who is intelligent or a night worker. From 'up north'. Rarely, a psychic or astrologer. Physically someone with flawless skin, delicate complexion or, with bad cards, psoriasis, eczema, a large birthmark, etc.

17. Storks.

Description: Describes someone as physically tall and long-legged and who, with cards 5, 8, 11 or 19, can have varicose veins or a bad gait due to leg trauma. With the Scythe an amputee. Someone who is an ambitious, restless soul working in the travel or real estate sectors.

Person: Woman, often older than the querent. Patron, mentor or honorary aunt.

18. Dog.

Description: Someone who is loyal, trustworthy, and who can act as an advocate on behalf of the querent and sometimes a doctor, nurse or vet. Dog owner. In legal questions, the querent's lawyer. Physically, a wide smile, doleful eyes; also often has a prominent tongue.

Person: Colleague, employee, business partner, friend or ally of either sex. In love, a man.

19. Tower.

Description: Physically, someone who is older than the querent, most often with greying hair, thin or tall. Someone who has been single (divorced, widowed) for a time. Unless by the Clouds, healthy, intelligent and protective influence.

Person: Father, grandfather, uncle. A male supervisor (not top boss).

20. Forest Garden.

Description: If after the person card, someone who is the 'queen bee' and elitist; otherwise, a social butterfly, people person, always out and about. Physically, it describes someone of medium height, well-dressed, and average to good looking.

21. Mountain.

Description: This is someone who is hateful towards the querent, difficult, cantankerous and often influential. Often racist. If the Garden, the Dog and the Child are by the significator and this is far away (from significator and bad cards), then an ally. Physically, this person is large-headed, muscular and has receding hair.

22. Paths.

Description: Physically, this is often someone at a 'special' age, e.g. 21, 40, 50, 65. Can have hair highlights, salt-and-paper hair or, occasionally, heterochromia. Also, someone who is in an open marriage or bisexual (with the Ring or the Lily, respectively, with both a 'split family'), divorced/remarried, has two homes due to working far away.

Person: Woman, similar age to the querent. Sibling. Helper. Backer. Advisor.

23. Mice.

Description: Someone who is small, rat-faced, often unkempt and rotten teeth. Past criminal record (minor, petty crimes). Has a passive-aggressive personality, dispirited and occasionally an emotional vampire.

24. Heart.

Description: This card describes someone beloved by the querent, always known. Characteristics include affectionate, happy, often gifted poet, eloquent.

25. Ring.

Description: To the left, someone you're contracted to/contracted to you, and to the right, someone you will be connected or contracted to. Otherwise, it indicates someone who is simply in a relationship with cards 5, 8, 11 and 19, suffers from a co-morbid or chronic health condition.

26. Book.

Description: If to the left of the person card, it is someone unknown to you, you've yet to meet them. Otherwise, intelligent, private, teacher or librarian.

27. Letter.

Description: When to the left of the person card, someone who is superficial and only connected to you fleetingly. Otherwise, someone you will hear about or from somewhere (telephone, email, letter) before you meet. Telecommunications worker.

30. Lily.

Description: Physically someone young, fair-haired, sexy and attractive, and muscular if male and voluptuous if female. Has an attentive personality, interested in social causes, occasionally able to offer patronage.

Person: Man, same age or younger. Adult male child if querent has several grandchildren.

31. Sun.

Description: Someone with blonde or reddish-gold hair, energetic, tanned or olive skinned, with a great physique. Can be from somewhere 'south' of the querent or a hot country. Characteristics include successful, flashy lifestyle, go-getter.

32. Moon.

Description: Classically good-looking, looks like and can occasionally be a famous person, Hollywood glamour, light blonde or platinum haired (but for men can actually be black). Part of a coterie and the querent's established social circle, works in the evening, successful job with company car, perks, credit card, etc.

33. Key.

Description: Does not add any physical descriptions, but indicates that the person is going to be exceptionally important or decisive in the querent's future. Otherwise, someone who is steadfast, true, lucky, a problem solver.

34. Fish.

Description: Normally indicates someone with green or blue eyes. Often has dark blonde or brown hair. Describes someone who is wealthy, a banker and lives a luxurious lifestyle.

Person: Man, similar age to querent. Sibling. Helper. Backer. Advisor.

35. Anchor.

Description: The Anchor is someone with a game plan; he or she has a clear idea of where he or she wants to be. With good cards, it shows someone who is faithful, monogamous, and who the querent hopes for help from or to find love with. Lives or is from the coast, has maritime or navy connections.

36. Cross.

Description: When this card is to the left of a person card, it can be someone the querent has not seen for several years or more. Otherwise, a religious person – rabbi, minister, Wiccan high priestess, imam, etc. To the right, someone down on luck, grieving, has chronic pain. Physically gangly, long arms and legs.

Appendix #2 – Health Combinations

It is impossible to avoid health combinations with the Petit Lenormand. The Tree will always show health issues or good health, and the Tower will always be lifelong or chronic issues and age. I found this out myself when I worked in the NHS for ten years. I had many clients who were doctors and nurses, and their patients' problems used to appear in readings when it was a serious or problematic case.

From these experiences, I derived the health and anatomical meanings given in this book.

You must be aware that you cannot legally perform diagnostic readings or give treatment based on the cards, be it physical, emotional or psychological. Should you even be qualified medically, if you have been consulted as a card reader, in most countries that would be classed as an inappropriate or illegal practice of medicine. Insurance and governance issues would also need to be considered. I include the following for illustrative purposes, and advise you that if you see them, consult a doctor or tactfully encourage your client to do so.

Please note, '/' denotes above.

GENERAL:

Tree: health in general.
Coffin: sickness.

Rod: aggravation, relapse, or repeating problems.

Tower: life, age.

TERMINAL:

Tower – Ship / Person – Cross – Coffin: terminal illness, normally known and in final stages.

OTORHINOLARYNGOLOGY (ENT) AND DENTISTRY:

Dog – Rod – Mountain: laryngitis.
Rod – Mountain: aphasia, mutism.
Rod – Birds – Coffin: earache.
Scythe – Dog – Paths: cut tongue, bleeding tongue.
Scythe – Dog – Mice: gum abscess, bad teeth.

OPHTHALMOLOGY:

Birds – Clouds – Lily: cataracts.
Clouds – Birds: short-sightedness.
Ship – Birds: long-sightedness.

NEUROLOGY:

Clouds – Lily/Book – Tower – Coffin: dementia.
Clouds – Book/Coffin: non-age related dementia, cognition difficulties.
Scythe – Paths – Mountain: cranial injury resulting in bleeding, such as a subdural haematoma.
Scythe – Paths – Fish – Mountain: cranial bleeding.
Coffin – Heart / Paths -- Mountain: cerebrovascular accident/stroke, i.e. interrupted blood flow.
Clouds – Book – Coffin: amnesia

PSYCHIATRY:

Clouds – Garden: mental health hospital.
Stars – Bear – Mountain: anorexia.
Stars – Bear – Rod: bulimia.
Clouds – Book – Lily: seasonal affective disorder.
Stars – Mountain: no sleep.

ONCOLOGY:

Moon – Mice – Tree: breast cancer.
Tree – Moon – Fish – Coffin: bladder cancer.
Tree – Clouds – Mice – Coffin: lung cancer.
Tree – Book – Mountain – Coffin: brain tumour.

CARDIAC:

Tree – Heart – Rod: tachycardia (very fast heart beat).
Heart – Sun – Key: ECG.
Scythe – Heart – Rod – Coffin: heart attack.
Heart – Birds: bradycardia (slow heart beat).
Scythe – Heart – Birds or Rod: high blood pressure.

GASTROENTEROLOGY:

Snake – Mice – Bear: parasites, tape worm.
Snake – Bear – Mice – Tree: Crohn's disease, colitis.
Snake – Bear – Bouquet – Coffin: ulcers.
Ship – Rod – Scythe: hiatal hernia.
Snake – Fish: diarrhoea.
Snake – Mountain: constipation.
Snake – Paths – Mountain: haemorrhoids.

ORTHOPAEDIC:

Scythe – Tower – Cavalier: slipped disc.
Scythe – Cavalier: ruptured ligament.
Scythe – Anchor: fractured neck or femur.

Lily – Letter – Mountain: arthritis in the hands.
Storks – Cavalier – Scythe: torn ligament.
Scythe – Cavalier – Coffin: broken leg or foot.
Letter – Rod: repetitive strain injury (hands).

DIABETES:

Ship – Mountain – Stars: diabetes.
Ship – Mountain – Stars – Bouquet – Mice: diabetic necrosis.

DERMATOLOGY:

Stars – Sun: eczema.
Scythe – Stars: open wound.
Scythe – Stars – Coffin (– Mice): infected tissue (necrotic tissue, gangrene).

PAEDIATRICS:

Child – Stars – Bouquet: chicken pox.
Child – Clouds – Bouquet: childhood asthma, allergies.
Child – Storks/Book: ADHD.
Child – Storks/Book – Mountain: autism.
Child – Cross/Stork: generalised childhood pains.
Child – Storks – Coffin or Tower: growing pains.

FEMALE AND MALE:

Scythe – Tower – either Fish or Moon: failure to reach sexual maturity for a man or woman, respectively.
Moon – Child – Mountain: low egg count.
Scythe – Moon – Child – Mountain: ectopic pregnancy.
Birds – Child: pregnancy.
Stork – Child – Cross: complicated birth, painful birth.
Lily – Fish – Mountain: low sperm count.

Lily – Fish – Coffin: male infertility.
Coffin – Moon – Rod (–Heart/Paths): menstrual problems (heavy bleeding).
Stars – Birds – Child – Key:IVF.
Birds – Child – Stars: healthy pregnancy, no worries.
Coffin – Birds – Child – Cross: stillbirth.
Scythe – Birds – Child – Coffin: abortion.
Scythe – Lady – Tower – Child: miscarriage.
Tree – Lady – Moon – Coffin: menopause.
Lady – Moon – Sun – Rod: hot flushes.

Person card – Lily – Garden – Mice: sexually transmitted disease.

HAEMATOLOGY:

Paths– Fish – Coffin: human immunodeficiency virus.
Paths– Fish – Coffin – Tower: acquired immunodeficiency syndrome.
Bear – Scythe – Paths: stomach bleeding.
Storks – Paths – Coffin: varicose veins.

GENERALISED AILMENTS:

Clouds – Bouquet – Coffin: hay fever.
Clouds – Garden – Scythe: a cold.
Rod/Clouds – Coffin – Scythe: the flu.
Scythe – Paths – Cavalier: road accident.
Tree – Fox – Coffin: not the right diagnosis, will get sicker.
Fox – Dog – Tree: wrong doctor.
Tree – Ring – Coffin: co-morbid conditions, the cards either side of the Tree and Coffin will say what.

TREATMENTS:

Coffin – Tree – Bouquet or Sun: improvement, will get better.

Coffin – Tree – Cross – Sun: full recovery.

Bouquet / Cavalier – Tree: improvement in health.

Bouquet – Cavalier – Key: treatment is working.

Clover – Bouquet – Book: holistic therapy.

Sun – Book – Key: Reiki.

Bouquet – Scythe – House: acupuncture.

Bouquet – Garden: convalescence.

Cavalier – Sun – House: resuming life, being ready to return to your affairs after treatment.

Appendix #3 – Playing Card Meanings & Multiples

Petit Lenormand is a method of reading playing cards. In readings of between three and fifteen cards, you may wish to note multiples of values, i.e. two kings, three aces, or four tens. These can provide a secondary reading that I have found to be accurate.

Kings:

4 – an honour (recognition).
3 – good counsel.
2 – favour (agreement, pronouncement).

Queens:

4 – negotiations, debates.
3 – a female rival.
2 – a female friend (either romantic or platonic, a woman helper).

Jacks:

4 – an outbreak (a household getting sick, or even an epidemic).
3 – disputes (often with a horrible man).
2 – disquiet in affairs (warning that things could go bad).

Tens:

4 – criminal record (a past).

3 – new station (new job, promotion).
2 – a change of scene (positive, holiday, move).

Nines:

4 – a trustworthy person, friend.
3 – success, green light.
2 – some money received.

Eights:

4 – reverse (a break up).
3 – a marriage.
2 – concord.

Sevens:

4 – plot (intrigue, gossip).
3 – ill health (for the client).
2 – tête-à-tête (being told minor news).

Sixes:

4 – strength (virility and health, feeling well).
3 – a lot of money.
2 – malicious actions.

Aces:

4 – fortune (good luck).
3 – moderate success.
2 – lies and deception.

Below I have included traditional meanings for the pips (playing card inserts), which can be used to provide a separate second separate. This are Swiss-German in origin.

HEARTS:

Querent's home, day-to-day life, affection. Spring.

Ace of Hearts (Lord) – building
King of Hearts (House) – male, querent.
Queen of Hearts (Storks) – female, querent.
Jack of Hearts (Heart) – querent's thoughts, desires.
10 of Hearts (Dog) – commitment.
9 of Hearts (Cavalier) – affections.
8 of Hearts (Moon) – certainties, wishes.
7 of Hearts (Tree) – emotions, well-being.
6 of Hearts (Stars) – friendships, connections.

SPADES:

Happiness, relationships, growth. Autumn.

Ace of Spades (Woman) – decision, news.
King of Spades (Lily) – young man, son.
Queen of Spades (Bouquet) – young woman, daughter.
Jack of Spades (Child) – thoughts or news of friends.
10 of Spades (Ship) – fortunate news.
9 of Spades (Anchor) – opportunity, investment.
8 of Spades (Garden) – visit, short-trip.
7 of Spades (Letter) – warning, consideration.
6 of Spades (Tower) – reflection, chance.

DIAMONDS:

Concerns, finances, precarious situations. Summer.

Ace of Diamonds (Sun) – answer, result.

King of Diamonds (Fish) – male, advisor.
Queen of Diamonds (Paths) – female, advisor.
Jack of Diamonds (Scythe) – revelation, risky development.
10 of Diamonds (Book) – big development, money.
9 of Diamonds (Coffin) – your money, solvency.
8 of Diamonds (Key) – victory, positive developments.
7 of Diamonds (Birds) – patience, hiatus.
6 of Diamonds (Clover) – surprise, small money.

CLUBS:

Problems, sickness and domination of the querent. Winter.

Ace of Clubs (Ring) – dread versus surprise
King of Clubs (Clouds) – older male relative, boss, someone with power over the querent
Queen of Clubs (Snake) – older female relative, boss, someone with power over the querent
Jack of Clubs (Rod) – querent's worries, fears
10 of Clubs (Bear) – aggression, anger
9 of Clubs (Fox) – strife, unpleasant surprise
8 of Clubs (Mountain) – pain, difficulties
7 of Clubs (Mice) – grief, tears
6 of Clubs (Cross) – secrets, lies

Appendix #4 – Timing

The following are cards that can indicate timing in a larger reading.

Coffin – Sun is sunrise.

Garden is at luncheon.

Garden – Moon is tea.

Moon – Stars is after dusk.

Moon – Child means at evening.

Moon is evening.

Stars is night.

Bouquet is spring.

Sun is morning and summer.

Scythe is autumn.

Lily is winter.

Letter – Paths is several days to two weeks.

Clover – Storks over Paths means by next week or next month.

Paths – Mice means a few weeks.

Paths – Clover is six weeks.

Clover – Paths is within three weeks.

Storks – Paths is within seven weeks.

Paths – Storks means changes in plans in a few weeks.

Paths – Mountain is delayed for several weeks.

Cross – Tower is in or after eight to twelve weeks' time.

Tree – Paths is more than two years.

Bear – Tree is within one or two decades.

Fox – Stars means incorrect timing, the timing is off.

Pace:

Whenever possible I recommend that you endeavour to use a time frame in your readings. One benefit of such practice is there are auguries that are more likely to occur in several months than several weeks.

Working in a time frame also allows a parameter that can be utilised to estimate timing further. We do this using pace of cards.

The thirty six cards in the deck can be divided into groups of three: fast-, middle- and slow-pace.

Here are the cards grouped by their pace:

Fast

Cavalier; Clover; Scythe; Child; Stars; Storks; Mice; Heart; Letter; Moon; Cross

Middle

Ship; House; Snake; Bouquet; Rod; Fox; Park; Paths; Ring; Man; Woman; Sun

Slow

Tree; Clouds; Coffin; Bear; Dog; Tower; Mountain; Book; Lily; Key; Fish; Anchor

'Pace' is derived from their core meanings. For example, you will see that the Clover, the Bouquet and the Lily are grouped in the fast, middle and slow categories respectively. Traditionally, all three of these cards deal with some form of happiness but the Clover is most fleeting (fast) while the Lily's happiness is fully sated (slow). In terms of love, the Heart is the initial flush of attraction (fast). It may progress to a relationship (Ring, middle) but only the Anchor says if it is last, or not (slow).

The pace of cards is the technique I use most, especially in readings such as lines of five, seven or nine and the 3 x 3. You first set your time-frame, and divide this into three.

Let us imagine we are doing a 3 x 3. This covers six weeks, at the most. Divided into three we can say fast cards would likely materialise within two weeks' time. Middle- and slow-paced cards would be indicate of within four and six weeks, respectively.

If we received:

> Ship – Anchor – Cavalier
> Clover – Woman – Sun
> Roads – Bouquet – Storks

We start by looking at predominance. Cavalier, Clover and Storks are all fast; the Anchor is the only slow-card. Four cards appear from the middle-pace. We could reasonably expect such as a reading, therefore, to play out within three to four weeks' time. Had there been no slow-card I would have said within two to four weeks' time.

The Seasonal System

The following is a very simple method of timing that utilises the significator. If the card representing the querent has appeared in the reading, look and see what card it faces. That card, as long as it is not an Ace, will give you the time period the events augured will effect.

If the significator has not appeared, go through the remaining cards that were not dealt as part of the reading and see what card the significator faces. You should not have the client reshuffle.

The Seasons:

As explained in the section concerning the four suits, each one is associated with a season:

Hearts stand for spring.
Diamonds are summer.
Spades are autumn.
Clubs are winter.

These associations are based on the Alemannic and Alsatian traditions of which the Petit Lenormand is part.

In this technique none of the four Aces has a time associated with it. This is because the card that gives you the timeframe is the card the significator faces. Obviously, depending on whether the querent is male or female, the significator will be either the Ace of Hearts (28 – the Lord) or the Ace of Spades (29 – the Lady).

The four sixes – that is the Stars, the Clover, the Tower, the Cross – can be seen as the start of the season. I find it useful, from a date perspective, to see them as the spring equinox, summer solstice, autumnal equinox and the winter solstice, respectively.

The four kings – the House, the Fish, the Lily and the Clouds – represent the end of the season.

Calculation:

I use the standard thirteen weeks, or 91 days, per season in this technique. Obviously we do not have thirteen cards in each suit. However, if you take each card as representing around eleven days you will have a good idea of an approximate time, which I have found is very accurate.

For example, the King of Hearts can be seen as the last eleven days of spring which would be June 9–20. In a reading for a woman, if the Lady faced the House card you can say the events discussed in her reading will take place at the latest by June 21. If the reading was done on December 1 2015 then it's June 21 2016.

The Garden, as the 8 of Spades, is approximately 25 October – 5 November (33 days after the start of autumn). If you were reading for a man, in April 2015, and the Lord faced the Garden, you can say that the events should have occurred by November 5 2015.

Appendix #5 – Grand Tableau Houses

Houses are a very popular method of reading with the Grand Tableau but I do not use them very often. There are so many techniques you can use with a Grand Tableau that if you use them all, you will muddle things for yourself. For me, proximity and attendance make up 90% of the reading. I do not mirror or knight unless I need to.

However, I will briefly demonstrate two of the seven house methods and how I use them, if I need to. In order to avoid potential confusion, I will call the two systems the Game of Hope and the Master Method houses.

Game of Hope Houses

Lenormand was originally a board game in which the cards were laid out in sequential order: 1 – Cavalier, 2 – Clover, 3 – Ship, 4 – House, 5 – Tree through to 36 – Cross. The Game of Hope houses imagines you are dealing the shuffled deck on such a board.

Based on this, the first card dealt in a Grand Tableau can be seen as occupying the position, or house, of the Cavalier. The fifteenth card dealt is in the house of the Bear (because the Bear is card 15). The last card dealt is in the house of the Cross.

<u>Interrupting the Houses:</u>

The card that is dealt into the house is thought to 'top' the house card, e.g. if the Bouquet was the first card dealt, it tops the Cavalier (so Cavalier + Bouquet).

Usage:

There is no rule for how one would work with the houses. You could read, starting from the Cavalier, each card in every house. Cards would be combined both with the houses and the card they fall to the right of.

For example, if the first three cards out were the Bouquet, the Ship and the Sun, these cards are in the houses of the Cavalier, the Clover and the Ship, respectively. You could, therefore, say:

You will have a visit from a woman (House of Cavalier + Bouquet) for a few days as part of her visit (House of Clover + Ship). She lives overseas (Bouquet + Ship). She will offer to return the favour (Bouquet + Ship + Sun) when you travel in the summer (House of the Ship + Sun).

Personally, that system does not work for me.

Important Houses:

If I were to use the houses, it would invariably be to look at what house the querent's card is in and what is in the house of the querent. It can also be worth checking what house the Clouds is in and what is in the house of the Clouds. This will show you where the biggest challenges are coming from.

Other important houses can be the Key and the Cross. The Key typically shows us certainties. The Cross increases the importance of whatever falls to its right. Consequently, anything in the position of the Cross is important both in terms of houses and as the last card. This is not a simple outcome, however. Seeing the Sun in the house of the Cross is not positive if it was far or the if Clouds sit directly above the Sun.

A lot of people will also check the house of the partner. Now, if you were reading for a woman who was in a relationship with a woman, you might take her partner to be the Snake. However, what house would be the partner's house? It is house 28, the Lord.

It's complicated, and it might not make much sense, but this is how it has worked for me. The reason is, the houses of the Lord and the Lady cards have no other meaning other than 'querent' and 'other person of significance'. In contrast, the house of the Snake invariably shows complications.

Game of Hope House Meanings

1. Cavalier: news, visitors.
2. Clover: improvement, companionship.
3. Ship: financial opportunities, travel.
4. House: home life, private life (behind closed doors).
5. Tree: health, past.
6. Clouds: problems, confusion.
7. Snake: complications, sedition.
8. Coffin: financial losses, sickness.
9. Bouquet: happiness, joy.

10. Scythe: danger, criminality.
11. Rod: strife, relapse.
12. Birds: upsets, trips.
13. Child: trust, children.
14. Fox: deceit, rivalry.
15. Bear: power, envy.
16. Stars: luck, clarity.
17. Storks: changes, movement.
18. Dog: friendship, loyalty.

19. Tower: life, time (long-term direction).
20. Forest Garden: society, networks.
21. Mountain: adversity, delays.
22. Paths: intersection, choices.
23. Mice: erosion, losses.
24. Heart: love, warmth.
25. Ring: relationships, partnerships.
26. Book: secrets, unknown.
27. Letter: telephone calls, communications.

28. Lord: querent, partner.
29. Lady: querent, partner.
30. Lily: ecstasy, family.
31. Sun: successes, growth.
32. Moon: job (day-to-day), reputation.
33. Key: certainties, future.
34. Fish: income, affluence.
35. Anchor: job (stability, career ambition), hopes.
36. Cross: hardship, full-top.

Master Method

The Master Method first appeared in the 1875 book *L'Oracle Parfait, Ou Le Passe Temps Des Dames: Art de Tirer Les Cartes Avec Explication*. The book attributed the method to Mademoiselle Le Normand. Again, there is no evidence to suggest she invented it or ever used it.

However, since then, it has been called variously Lenormand's Nines and Lenormand's Houses. Due to the association with Mlle Le Normand, the method has been adapted by several readers for the Petit Lenormand.

The original method uses 36 playing cards. The cards are shuffled, cut and dealt out in four rows of nine. You read the cards touching the significator and then each card individually by house. Each house has a meaning, such as Project, or Marriage, or Good Fortune. Each house further carries a meaning depending on the suit of the card that is dealt there. For example, seeing a spade card in the fourteenth house augurs having one's affections thwarted, but with the promise of overcoming this through faithfulness and patience.

Below are the house meanings that I translated from French. Where necessary, I have elaborated to avoid confusion.

Master Method House Meanings

1. Projects.

2. Satisfaction.
3. Success.
4. Expectations.
5. Chance [risk taking, speculation].
6. Desires.
7. Injustice [negative events without perceived cause].
8. Ingratitude [rejection, refusals].
9. Friendships [friendships, networking].

10. Losses [of possessions, interests].
11. Hurt.
12. Estate [possessions, investments, dividends].
13. Joy.
14. Love [affairs of the heart].
15. Prosperity [financial and material luck].
16. Marriage [commitment, ties usually romantic].
17. Upsets [worries, sorrow].
18. Enjoyment.

19. Inheritance [gifts, money not earned from work].
20. Betrayal.
21. Rivalry [conflict of interest, competition].
22. Gifts.
23. Lover [the significant other].
24. Promotion [betterment, improving yourself or your situation].
25. Benefit [agreement, pact].
26. Enterprise [undertaking].
27. Changes.

28. Endings.
29. Rewards [salary, payment].
30. Disrepute [loss of reputation, questionable actions].
31. Happiness.

32. Wealth.
33. Indifference [inattention, apathy in affairs].
34. Benefits [advantage through another person or skill].
35. Ambitions [goals, end sight].
36. Indisposition [sickness, being held back by circumstances].

Usage:

For use with the Petit Lenormand rather than noting the suit, readers use the cards' meanings. As an example, we will return to George's Grand Tableau and look at the Lord and cards around the Lord.

The Storks are in the house (1) of purpose. This shows us that the relocation and the changes George is making are done for a reason. These are calculated changes with an end goal in sight.

George's card, the Lord, is in the house (2) of satisfaction. These changes are designed to bring George what he wants. If he pulls them off, he will be very satisfied and receive a step up (Storks + Lord).

Now, we reach the Moon, which is in the house (3) of success. Professionally, George is about to make a great achievement for all to see just how well he has done (Lord + Moon).

Below the Storks is the House. This has fallen in the house (9) of friendships. He is going to be careful about whom he invites indoors. With the Storks above it, he is consciously thinking about the neighbourhood he wants to relocate to.

In the house (10) of losses, we find the Ship. George is conscious that by moving on, he will have to leave behind his current neighbourhood (House + Ship).

We find the Key in the house (11) of hurt. Moving (Ship + Key) is sure to hurt!

Both of these systems work. Both have their strong fan base. As you grow in proficiency, you will be able to experiment with this or any system. However, I have genuinely found that less is very often more. Thus, I would counsel you to exercise some common sense. You do not need to do everything.

Appendix #6 – Learning Resources

Online Resources

There are numerous online Lenormand resources. For conceptual clarity, few match the videos of international fortune teller and astrologer, Malkiel Rouven Dietrich. Dietrich is Europe's Lenormand expert. In addition, the German psychic Hexe Claire's videos are immensely and justly popular.

Videos:

Dietrich, M. R. (2015). Malkiel Rouven Dietrich. [online] YouTube. Available at: http://www.youtube.com/user/MyMalkiel

Hexe Claire. (2015). Hexe Claire [online] YouTube. Available at: http://www.youtube.com/user/hexeclairechannel

Websites:

Stella Waldvogel's blog contains practical, straight-talking advice: http://www.fennario.wordpress.com

Lenormand Cards Study Group has an international membership: http://www.facebook.com/groups/LenormandCardStudy/

Lauren Forestell restores antique Lenormand decks and offers downloads of historical Lenormand instructions, including the Philippe Lenormand sheet:
http://www.gameofhopelenormand.bigcartel.com

The Tarot Association of the British Isles forum has a Lenormand section:
http://www.tabi.org.uk

Both Café Lenormand (www.cafelenormand.com) and "Lord Ewin's" Learn Lenormand (http://www.learnlenormand.com) contain a lot of useful information.

Books

English:

Dos Ventos, M. (2007). The Game of Destiny: Fortune Telling with Lenormand Cards. London: Nzo Quimbanda Exu Ventania, p. 212.
Katz, M. and Goodwin, T. (2013). Learning Lenormand. Minnesota: Llewellyn Publications, p. 312.
George, R. (2014). The Essential Lenormand: Your Guide to Precise & Practical Fortunetelling. Minnesota: Llewellyn, p.408.
Matthews, C. (2014). The Complete Lenormand Oracle Handbook: Reading the Language and Symbols of the Cards. Vermont: Destiny Books, p. 416.

French:

Marco, M. (1999). Petit Lenormand: Méthode de cartomancie. Brussels: Servranx, p.224.

Ripert, P. (2008). Les tarots de Mlle Lenormand. Paris: De Vecchi, p. 137.

Silvestre, C. (2003). Le Petit Lenormand. Montpellier: Editions du Gange, p. 206.

German:

Treppner, I. (2010). Die Sibylle der Salons: Das Lenormand-Praxisbuch für Menschen von heute. München: Heyne Verlag, p. 272.

Droesbeke von Enge, E. (1988). Das Orakel der Mlle Lenormand. Neuhausen: AGM Urania, p. 174.

Appendix #7 – Translation of the 'Philippe Lenormand' Meanings

The following is a translation of the meanings given to the cards in the original instructions, after they were re-named 'Lenormand', circa 1850. This is the sheet often referred to as the 'Philippe Lenormand instructions'. Originally in German it was translated into Dutch, French and English, as well as being exported to Eastern Europe, South America and Scandinavia, with 98 % of Petit Lenormand decks, between the years 1850 – 1930.

--

Shuffle the cards well and cut them and then arrange them in five parts or rows, the first four of which are composed of eight cards and the fifth one of only four. The first row commences on the left, as do the second, third and fourth rows below, with the last four cards placed underneath in the middle, as shown in the diagram below:

00 – 00 – 00 – 00 – 00 – 00 – 00 – 00
00 – 00 – 00 – 00 – 00 – 00 – 00 – 00
00 – 00 – 00 – 00 – 00 – 00 – 00 – 00
00 – 00 – 00 – 00 – 00 – 00 – 00 – 00
** – ** – 00 – 00 – 00 – 00 – ** – **

The person who wishes to know their future is shown by Nr. 28, if they are man or a boy, and by Nr. 29 [1], if they are woman or a girl. It is upon these two cards, Nr. 28 and Nr. 29, that attention must be focussed, for it is by their position in the game that future happiness or misfortune depends. The remaining cards receive their meanings from them, based on their distance from these two cards, fixing destiny.

Explanation of the Cards:

1. Cavalier, indicates good news, but a little far away, it can relate to the person's home or come from foreign countries. This card is a messenger of good fortune when it is not surrounded by cards of a sinister nature.

2. Clover, brings luck, but if surrounded by clouds it is an omen of many sorrows; if this card is near to the one that represents the person, the sorrow will not last for long and there will be a happy ending.

3. Ship, indicates wealth obtained by commerce or by inheritance; it also means travel when it is located near the person.

4. House, signifies success and prosperity in all enterprises, even if the present situation of the person is unfortunate, he can expect a better future. If this card is located in the middle of the game, below the person, it is a warning to be on their guard regarding their surroundings.

5. Tree, away from the person, it is a sign of good health, several trees together there is no doubt that their wishes will be fulfilled and they will have brilliant future.

6, Clouds, when the light side faces the person, it is a happy sign, but if it is the dark side, then some problem will soon appear.

7, Snake, is a sign of misfortunes, which is gauged by the distance of the card to that of person, but always brings hypocrisy, betrayal and loss.

8. Coffin, close to the person, signifies chronic serious illness, death and the loss of all fortune. When away from the person card it is less dangerous.

9. Bouquet of Flowers signifies happiness in all areas.

10. Scythe, omen of great danger which can be avoided when surrounded by good cards.

11. Rod, signifies family quarrels and domestic trouble, dissension between spouses, fever and long illness.

12. Birds, signifies troubles that we will have to endure, but only for a short time. Far from the person this card is a sign of happy journey.

13. Child, is a sign that you have good support, are full of goodness, and well regarded within the world.

14. Fox, if this card is near, you must beware of those with whom you are connected, because some seek to deceive you, otherwise there is no danger.

15. Bear, signifies happiness, but warns of the need to avoid conversations with those who envy.

16. Star, confirms good luck in all your enterprises, but if it surrounded by clouds, it indicates a long period of misfortune.

17. Stork, close to a person, it indicates a chance of the current home, at a distance the change is delayed.

18. Dog, very close, it is an assurance of fidelity and friendship; very far it indicates betrayal, and if surrounded by clouds it warns not to rely on those who call themselves friends.

19 Tower, announces a long life and a happy old age; but if it surrounded by clouds, it announces sickness, and in certain circumstances, even death.

20 Forest Garden, announces good company, which you will soon enter, and when near it assures, again, a constant friendship; but far away, it is a sign of false friends.

21. Mountain, near to the person, warns you to fear a powerful enemy, but when far away you can rely on influential friends.

22. Paths, surrounded by clouds it is a sign of unhappiness, but away from this card [2] and the person, there are ways or means to be found to escape a danger

23. Mice, is a sign of theft, if it is near to the person, one will be able to recover what was taken; but if it is far away, the loss is irreversible.

24. Heart, is a sign of joy, happiness and of unity.

25. Ring, on the right of the person it announces a happy and brilliant[3] marriage, but if far and to the left, it announces the separation of two loves.

26. Book, communicates a secret, and its position allows us to judge what it concerns; however, we must proceed with caution in this regard.

27. Letter, without clouds this is sign that happiness will be derived from pleasant news coming from a distance; but if clouds are located in the vicinity of the person, they must expect many sorrows.

28. Lord, is the dominant card in the game, along with card nr. 29, and shows us the happiness or misery of the person consulting the cards.

29. Lady, is of the same importance, as all is revealed according to its position in the game, despite the perspicacity of the person reading the cards.

30. Lily, announces a happy life unless surrounded by clouds where it indicates sorrows in the family. If this card is found above the person it indicates virtue, below, it cast doubts on their principles.

31. Sun, near, you are enlightened by its rays and happiness grows, but if it is far away, all cools with discouragement in all enterprises and prepares [4] for calamities.

32. Moon, is a sign of great honour, if this card is locate next to the person, on the contrary, if it is at a distance it announces misfortunes.

33. Key, when near it announces the successful end of a matter, but at a distance the opposite.

34. Fish, prepares you to make a fortune by the sea, and series of happy enterprises; but if they are removed from the person, they are a sinister omen of the best of your projects being reversed.

35. Anchor, is the sign of a successful enterprise at sea, and a great advantage in commerce and of a faithful love; but if at a distance indicates a total error in your ideas and love that proves fickle [5].

36. Cross, is always an ill omen, however, if it is very close to the person, it is such that the misfortune will not be long-lasting.

[1] Instructions incorrectly associate Nr. 28 with the Lady and Nr. 29 with the Lord.

[2] It is believed that this means if the Clouds is 'away' (far) from the Paths and the person, but the originally text is such that it could easily be if the Paths are away from both the Clouds and person card.

[3] The original wording implies either a dowry or a marriage that proves prosperous, financially.

[4] 'prepares for calamities' refers to the Sun making a prediction of future difficulties.

[5] The text refers to 'papillon' which means 'butterfly' but is an expression of fleetingness, someone or something fickle.

Appendix #8 - Decks

There are many Petit Lenormand decks available now, and the Internet has made it far easier to obtain a wide variety of styles. However, you do not need to own a Petit Lenormand deck to read with the method outlined in this book.

A Schafkopf Tarock (German set of 36 playing cards) deck can be used. Similarly, a regular poker deck can be adapted – just remove the twos, threes, fours, fives and Jokers. A permanent marker to write the cards' names on your adapted deck is useful if you are a new student.

If you want a set of special cards I recommend the following:

Classic Lenormands:

Ur-Lenormand: Das Spiel der Hoffnung (Königsfurt-Urania – reproduction of the first Petit Lenormand).

Lenormand Orakelkarten – Blaue Eule (Königsfurt-Urania – playing card insets, German instructions, has a blue owl on the back).

Lenormand Orakelkartenmit Kartenabbildungen (Königsfurt-Urania – modern version of the deck used in this book, German instructions).

Jeu Lenormand Cartes de Bonne Aventure (Carta Mundi – available with French, Dutch or German rhymes).

No. 194115 Mlle Lenormand (Piatnik – playing card insets, Italian, German, English, French instructions).

ASS Lenormand: Die echten Altenburg-Spielkarten (Königsfurt-Urania – playing card inserts or German verses, German instructions).

Modern Lenormands:

Gilded Reverie Lenormand (US Games Systems, Inc – modern deck with detailed fantastical designs by Ciro Marchetti).

The Maybe Lenormand (US Games Systems, Inc – a breathtaking, contemporary but traditional deck by the gifted artist and reader Ryan Edward – please note, the deck's name may change upon publication).

The Enchanted Lenormand Oracle (Watkins Publishing Ltd – comes with a book by Caitlín Matthews and cards by Virginia Lee).

Lenormand Oracle Cards (Lo Scarabeo – no playing card inserts or verse, Italian, German, Spanish, English and French instructions).

Mystical Lenormand (Königsfurt-Urania – detailed but sometimes cryptic designs painted in egg tempera).

Celtic Lenormand (US Games Systems, Inc – modern deck with a pagan theme).

The Egyptian Lenormand (Schiffer Publishing Ltd – modern deck drawing on the rich legacy of Ancient Egypt).

Appendix #9 – Combination Readings

I am frequently asked by students and fellow Lenormand enthusiasts whether you can combine the Petit Lenormand with other reading methods. The answer is, of course you can. You can do whatever you want. The question you should ask is why you would want to do it and if it would meet your needs.

The majority of the people who ask are already card readers. Usually, they are readers of the tarot. It is invariably the tarot that they want to combine with the Petit Lenormand.

And yes, this is doable. But first let us ponder a few considerations. The tarot is a set of playing cards comprised, in its most usual form, of twenty-one trumps, a folly-card (known as the greater arcana), and fifty-six pip cards (known as the lesser arcana). Pip cards is another word for suited playing cards. And what is the Petit Lenormand? A set of pip cards.

For this reason, I ask those interested in pursuing such a combination if they really need the tarot's pip cards when they have the Petit Lenormand. Many are horrified at the idea of not using the tarot's pips. In continental Europe, many tarot readers only use the twenty-one trumps and folly-card.

Some who do use the pips often strip them, so that the number matches the common number of cards used in 'regular' cartomancy. One reader I know has done this as she uses Etteilla's meanings for a thirty-two card pack with her tarot's pips.

When I use the tarot, unless I need more than ten cards, I use only the trumps and folly-card. I would thus not see a need to use the pips if I were going to do a reading with the Petit Lenormand also. And when I have tried this, I have done two separate readings.

For me tarot is an optical system. Petit Lenormand is an emblematic system. With tarot, I am heavily concerned with the visual flow of the cards' symbolic designs from one to the other.

However, when I do combine the Petit Lenormand with another discipline, I prefer not to use cards, but astrology; horary astrology, to be exact. Horary (i.e. the hour) is an ancient reading technique used to answer specific questions by casting a chart for the time a question is asked and understood. It works best with questions that are verifiable.

My mode of working is to cast a horary chart and then, pondering the answer, to deal cards. I find the two do work well together. Often, the horary gives me the answer and tactical insight that can further hone or direct (i.e. give further context) my readings of cards.

Example Reading:

Below is a reading I did in August 2013. I had been unwell and received treatment which made reading for clients difficult. Thus, my private consultancy work had provided a useful supplement to my earning during my recuperation. Yet, I had learnt that a need to economise meant that my services might not be needed due to my fees.

My question for the horary chart was: Will I stay in role? I noted the time I thought that, and the chart was cast for the time at which that question seriously entered my head.

The chart:

Chart: Morinus Traditional
[http://sites.google.com/site/tradmorinus/morinus]

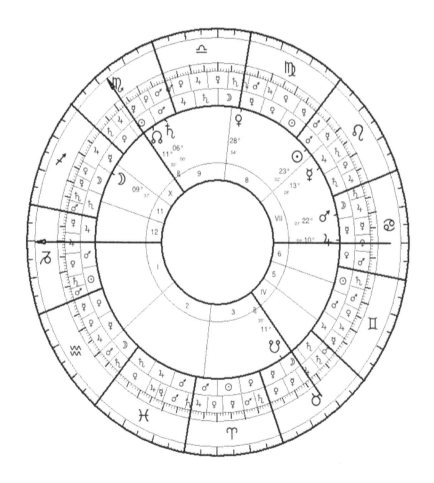

The querent – me, in this instance – is represented by the ascending sign and, more explicitly, by the ruler of the ascendant. Capricorn is rising, and that means Saturn represents me in this chart. Saturn is in Scorpio in the ninth house and, unfortunately, is peregrine, which means he is without any essential dignity (a serious debility in traditional astrology). The ninth house rules, amongst other things, professionals, so that makes sense here, and Saturn is conjunct by orb to the North Node, an indicator of gain, which is a little odd.

Our next significator is the quesited – the topic about which I am asking – and this is represented by the tenth house, as that rules one's employment. Scorpio is on the tenth, which means the job is represented by Mars. Mars is in Cancer and also peregrine. He is in the seventh house. The seventh house signifies 'the other person', be it a spouse or known enemies, so the job at the moment is with another person.

Now we return to the question. Traditional signs of keeping a role is finding the lord of the tenth in the first house (not seen here) and seeing the lords of the first and tenth in an angular house (1, 4, 7, 10). Saturn is in a cadent house (3, 6, 9, 12). Mars is angular but debilitated and would be leaving Cancer soon, a sign of departure.

I calculated the Greek Lot (or Arabic Part) of dismissal. This fell at 23° Virgo and was thus ruled by Mercury. Mercury was squaring (tense aspect) Saturn (me) whilst the Moon (other person) was trining (easy aspect) Mercury. Mars was also aspecting the actual degree of the Lot.

My overall feeling, based on my experience, was that the answer was no. The aspect between Saturn and Mercury was a separating one, which symbolised the decision had already been made. I now wanted to know where I should look for avenues to make up this potential loss of income.

The Petit Lenormand was perfect for this. Focusing on the chart's revelations, I shuffled my Petit Lenormand and dealt a 3 x 3.

As discussed before, if I deal nine cards, I expect that at least one key topic card will appear. Both the Fish (money) and the Ship (financial opportunities, self-employment) appeared. The cards were also very positive. This reminded me of the North Node close to the tenth house.

The cards as they fell:

Cross – Cavalier – Fish
Ship – Sun – Birds
Garden – House – Stars

The Cross coming out first echoes my concerns about potential hardship but the corners show that after testing times (Cross) my finances (Fish) would grow and expand with my clientele (Garden – Stars).

There will be difficult (Cross) news (Cavalier) about my finances. The Cavalier – Fish falling after the Cross, however, is promising but emphasises that I need to take action. There will be at least two (Birds) financial opportunities to explore (Ship – Sun). These lie with expanding (Garden) my fortune-telling business (House – Stars).

To overcome the difficulties (Cross), I would need to move (Ship) my focus to widening my clientele (Garden). Ship – Garden told me, also, to be prepared to travel more to meet with clients, or to do events. This also echoed Saturn (me, in the horary chart) being in the house of distant travel. Cavalier – Sun – House told me that I was ready to resume my daily living activities. I had sufficient energy and stamina. So despite some financial worries (Fish – Bird) I was more than capable of finding (Stars) a way to supplement (Fish – Birds = two sources of income) my earnings.

Cross – Sun – Stars promised me that I would successfully overcome any hardship. Fish – Sun – Garden told me that I would find financial success in events and groups.

The following day my impression of the horary chart was confirmed. I heard almost to the minute when Mars perfected (reached the exact degree of) his aspect to the Lot of Dismissal. By that time, I had already booked readings in Bridgnorth and London. I had not been planning to visit clients there, but knew I needed the money. I had also ordered new business cards, and a few weeks later started to do readings at parties and events which I had previously been reluctant to do. Late the following evening, I had a call from a friend who asked me to come and talk at a small spiritualist group.

The readings at parties and the talks have now become two regular additions to my business ventures.

All in all, my business benefited from not doing governance work at that time. In the horary chart, this was shown by the North Node near to both Saturn and the tenth house cusp. In the Petit Lenormand, the Sun and the Stars are near the house. Both the horary chart and the 3 x 3 echoed each other but helped to contextualise each other in a way that one alone might not have done. I am doubtful tarot combined with the Petit Lenormand would have done so.

If you ever combine methods, you want to have two distinct disciplines that will complement each other and not duplicate.

Appendix #10 - Mademoiselle Marie-Anne Le Normand

Marie-Anne Adelaide Le Normand* was born and baptised on 27 May 1772, in Alençon, Normandy. Shortly after her death a hostile biographer posted an earlier date of birth. However, parish records in Alençon show she was born the third child and second daughter of Jean Louis Antoine Le Normand and Marie-Anne Gilbert in 1772.

Jean Louis was a draper who died a year after his daughter's birth. Left with three children, Marie-Anne Gilbert remarried, then died herself before her daughter turned five. Her stepfather placed Marie-Anne and her older sister in a Benedictine Convent for their education, moving them later to the Order of the Visitation. Le Normand was very clever and precocious, and the education that she received was clearly of some merit. Later she showed a head for figures that was quite remarkable. The popular myth that Le Normand predicted the replacement of an abbess during this time is not supported by the Order's records.

When Mademoiselle Le Normand was still a teenager she moved from Normandy to Paris, where she was made an apprentice dressmaker. It was at this time she is said to have encountered a woman named Madame Gilbert, who could have been a maternal relative. Madame Gilbert introduced Le Normand to cartomancy.

Tradition holds that Mlle Le Normand acquired Etteilla's Manière de se récréer avec le jeu de cartesnommées tarots. However, from her own writings and those of her clients, it is clear that if Le Normand did commence her apprenticeship with the Etteilla method then she did not continue with it.

Once the Revolution began, Le Normand was quick to try to remain on the good side of the new powers. She failed, and was eventually arrested and taken to la Force prison at the height of the Terror; not for being part of the resistance, as she later claimed, but for fortune-telling.

It was during this time that Le Normand first became linked to the former Marié Josephe Rose de La Pagerie, later the Empress Josephine. It is said that Marié Josephe sent a message to Le Normand to enquire about her estranged husband's fate. Le Normand said he would die, but that Marié Joseph would not, and would make a second, more brilliant match.

MariéJosephe's son Eugene recorded in his memoirs how he and his sister, Hortense, ran messages between their mother and several others during the Terror. Marié Josephe was known to use psychics and fortune-tellers, an interest shared by her friend, the Russian Emperor Alexander. We do not know how often MariéJosephe consulted Le Normand, but all of the Empress' modern biographers accept that she did.

It was the end of the Terror, and the move towards the Empire, that marked the start of the impressive accession of Le Normand's fortunes. It seemed to centre more on her association with the fate of several men than Marié Josephe. Le Normand had – or the populace believed she had – predicted the deaths of St Just, Marat, and others. Thus she became a rising star in the beginnings of the Empire, becoming a wealthy woman in her own right.

Some have cast doubt on the level of her fame. But this ignores the writings of independent clients and diarists, French and otherwise, and the newspapers that covered her death. All attest to her celebrity. The remarkable queues outside her home (marked 'Librarie' for legal reasons), the scale of her funeral, and the newspaper columns devoted to her all say she was a very famous fortune-teller.

Wealth allowed Le Normand to aid her siblings. She arranged a marriage for her sister and sponsored her brother's military career. Both died young, to Le Normand's grief. Le Normand took on the responsibility of looking after her sister's son, Michel-Alexandre Hugo, her only close relative, who entered military service.

Just as she did not use the Petit Etteilla, neither did she invent the Petit Lenormand. The cards were invented by the German, Johann KasparHechtel, and began their life as a German racing game called Das Spiel der Hoffnung, or The Game of Hope. They were only relabelled 'Petit Lenormand' after Marie-Anne Le Normand's death.

In Les Oracles Sibyllins (1817), Le Normand describes two readings she did. The first is with tarot cards (that appear to be Marseilles-styled, not Etteilla), and the second using a 32-card pack, as in the game of piquet. The closest match, in terms of meanings to Le Normand's summarisation, is in the parlour tradition, which was the basis for J.J. Grandville's Le Livre du Destin.Even those who wrote about Le Normand using several decks do not describe The Game of Hope.

Le Normand died on 25 June 1843. She was buried two days later at the Cimetière du Père-Lachaise after a lavish funeral. Her grave is regularly maintained and visited by modern card readers from France and other countries.

* During her lifetime Mlle Le Normand did sign her surname as 'Le Normand'. We have several extant examples of her handwriting. After her death, her heir, Lieut Michel-Alexandre Hugo, distanced himself from his aunt's trade and denounced her so-called successors as well as decks that carried her name.

Sources:

Le Normand - Les souvenirs prophétiquesd'unesibyllesur les causes secrétes de son arrestation (1814)
Le Normand - Les oracles sibyllinsou la suite des souvenirs prophétiques (1817)
Memoirs of Karl August von Malchus - The Dublin University Magazine, vol. 30
Decker, Depaulis, Dummett - A Wicked Pack of Cards: The Origins of the Occult Tarot (1996)
Williams - Josephine: Desire, Ambition, Napoleon (2013)
Erickson - Josephine: A Life of the Empress(2004)
Hibbert - The French Revolution (1982)

Various – Musée national des châteaux de Malmaison et Bois-Préau (2006)

Johns - Empress Josephine's collection of sculpture by Canova at Malmaison (Journal of the Historical Collections, May 2004)

Rey & Emanuel - Alexander I: The Tsar Who Defeated Napoleon (2012)

Hall - Napoleon's Letters to Josephine 1796-1814 (2010)

Andy Boroveshengra

Andy Boroveshengra is a professional fortune-teller and tutor living and working in the United Kingdom. He specialises in palmistry, which he learnt from his Rromni mother and her Roma family, but also reads with the Petit Lenormand and traditional tarot.

He is a Tarot Association of the British Isles (TABI) endorsed reader, and has acted as a tutor for TABI for the last two years.

In June 2015, Andy launched his one-to-one tutoring programme on reading the Petit Lenormand. A tarot programme is due in August 2015.

Andy lives in the West Midlands with his dogs and cats, and also reads regularly in Mayfair, London.

.

Andy Boroveshengra
palmist — card reader — tutor

http://www.boroveshengra.com/

Made in the USA
Las Vegas, NV
18 April 2024